THE

CITY

IS THE

PEOPLE

VIEW OF TOLEDO

HENRY S. CHURCHILL

THE
CITY
IS THE
PEOPLE

With a new Preface and Epilogue

The Norton Library
W · W · NORTON & COMPANY · INC ·
NEW YORK

FIRST PUBLISHED IN THE NORTON LIBRARY 1962

By arrangement with Harcourt, Brace & World, Inc.

Books That Live
The Norton imprint on a book means that in the publisher's
estimation it is a book not for a single season but for the years.
W. W. Norton & Company, Inc.

SBN   393   00174   1

Printed in the United States of America

4 5 6 7 8 9 0

PREFACE

Fifteen years and more have passed since this little book was written. It is with satisfaction that I see it reprinted, for on reading it over, which I had not done for some years, I find it contains if not wisdom at least sound observation.

During the intervening years I have been occupied with the practice of city-planning, either as a bureaucrat or as a "consultant" or as a critic. I have changed my mind about a good many things I said in 1945. I am not sure in what category these revisions place me, that of senile conservationist or rejuvenated reactionary. It probably does not matter. What does matter, I believe, is that nearly all my contemporaries and most of my juniors still have the same ideas they had twenty years ago.

I have not changed my mind about the basic thesis that it is people who make a city. On the contrary, what concerns me today is the perversion of planning methods and processes from democratic community organization to authoritarian controls for the benefit of a few. I cannot look with equanimity on technocratic infallibility as a measure of men's needs. I am no Utopian.

My fears are perhaps exaggerated. So far, at least, the technocratic controls—both physical and economic—which have been legislated have been broken down by the ingenuity of the private speculator and the practical politician working hand-in-pocketbook. This is a salutary thought. It has always been easier to correct the excesses of political corruption than the excesses of uncorruptible self-righteousness.

In any case planning is here to stay, which makes it all the more necessary to re-examine some of our planning clichés— or, if you prefer, our planning ideals and goals. Is Urban Sprawl as bad as it is said to be? Bad for whom, and why? To what extent is physical obsolescence due to economic changes and, conversely, to what extent does economic deterioration derive from physical deterioration? Are not slums entirely economic phenomena, physical only in manifestation? If so, we are wasting effort in "clearing" them. What is "blight?" What amuses people and attracts them to places? Certainly not "Art" and "Cultcha."

There are many other questions. If the planners would look around they would be surprised at how unreal are some of their cherished assumptions and how foolish is much of their conventional wisdom.

What is astonishing is the now almost complete acceptance of this conventional planning wisdom. This acceptance is found not only in technical circles, but in administrative ones, and to a large degree in popular ones. Planning is no longer Socialism, it is Panacea. Zoning is well-nigh universal; the words "Comprehensive Plan" soothe the judicial breast when anything is in accord with whatever it is. The 5-year Budget was not invented by Stalin but by conservative accountants of Big Business. We are to have a Department of Urban Affairs. And so it goes. This is all to the good, this is progress. The acceptance of ideas as conventional wisdom is a pre-condition to the acceptance of further ideas. It is important, therefore, that always new ideas be forthcoming.

New ideas are generated by the fresh observation of old facts. "Facts" are not just bundles of statistical data; facts are experiences of things as commonly accepted by people. They may be interpreted in different ways, given new insights. This has nothing to do with quantification or datafication, which serve only for justification. The figures remain the same, but somehow the object looks different. Sometimes this can be done just by the distortion of a mirror from concave to convex or *vice versa*. This is likely to break the mirror, which causes academic scandal and bureaucratic ill-will. Consequently it is seldom done.

It is probable that the notable lack of success of the large-scale planning program jocosely called "urban renewal" will at least stimulate new thought and new ideas. So will the gradual passing out of the academic picture of the older men such as myself. There are signs on the horizon of new concepts in physical planning and of new thinking. Among the leaders, to name some but not all (saving clause!) are William L. C. Wheaton, Jean Gottmann, Henry Fagin, Herbert Gans, Victor Gruen . . .

To these, and to others, it is clear that what we have to deal with is no longer the old City, but something quite other. If the city in history looks backwards megalopolis looks forward. The city is still the people.

Henry S. Churchill

Philadelphia, January, 1962

TO THE MEMORY OF

HENRY WRIGHT

CONTENTS

ILLUSTRATIONS

ILLUSTRATIONS

Finis. Photo by Tet Borsig.

THE
CITY
IS THE
PEOPLE

1. ANTECEDENTS

W E ARE ON THE THRESHOLD OF A CRUCIAL ERA OF change in the urban way of life. Vast disintegrating and destructive forces are loose in the world; but also, almost for the first time, there is a common consciousness that these forces can be turned to the constructive uses of the community. We are seeking new physical urban settings just as we are seeking new social and economic patterns.

There is endless talk of "urban redevelopment," and "Master planning," and "stopping the spread of blight," and "the process of decentralization." There is little understanding of the processes at work, of the historical continuity of our urbanism. "The more things change, the more they remain the same." The forces for change are relentless, the human aspirations remain the same. New forces are at work, which are incomprehensible except in terms of the past, if only for contrast, and are perhaps unpredictable on any score. The inability to predict should not make us fear understanding, rather it should make us seek it, for if we are to replan our cities we must know what it is that changes and why.

Trade and exchange are what have formed cities. They have been located wherever natural trade routes crossed, wherever strategic strong points have been available: Cnossos, cross-roads of the Egean Sea; Mohenjo-daro, in the ancient Indus Valley;

Babylon and Bagdad; Bokhara and Kiev; Cairo, Athens, Rome, London, Paris, New York, Chicago, Juneau—on the rivers, estuaries and seas, dominating trade routes at valley intersections, at places where transhipment was natural, along the silk road, along the railroad. Similarly, the lesser cities, local market places growing up where roads crossed, where fertile valleys produced and streams turned mills.

The ideas exchanged were as important as the goods traded. Only in cities, where the clash of thought has sharpened wits, where surplus wealth has permitted leisure, and where the power of wealth has provided safety, has there been progress and civilization. This was true from the beginning of cities:

> In cities the social process was given a new form. A far larger number of individuals than ever dwelt in villages lived in continuous association with one another; the city was a vortex of social interaction. Objects and commodities from widely separated regions were brought together, permitting the making of new combinations of materials. Strange men came, bearing not only foreign wares but also new bits of information and unknown beliefs. And old acquaintances met often, to talk over both the old and the new things they heard. This constant inter-stimulation in the presence of considerable material wealth moved men to produce more of it and also to acquire and hold it; this wealth also made possible the release of energies in enterprises other than those of obtaining subsistence. Thus the city became a center of economic advance, social specialization, artistic creation, and intellectual innovation, and new social relations rooted in these developments worked themselves into new political and economic institutions and ethical judgments.[1]

According to the archeologists, city planning has existed since the first cities known to man: the river-flat cities of the Indus, the Euphrates and the Nile Valleys 2000 to 3000 B.C. There had to be planning even in those remote times, because planning,

[1] *The Great Cultural Traditions*, Rise of Urban Culture in Mesopotamia and India. Dr. Ralph Turner. McGraw-Hill, 1941.

which is only another name for social control over the use of land, arose from the need of maintaining social, political, and economic order among large groups of people living in close proximity. Among the nomad tribes there was no need for planning, the steppes were vast enough for the pitching of tents. The continual search for pasture-lands and the consequent need for conquest provided them with a social and political organization of an eminently "practical" sort, but it was neither urban nor urbane. The wanderers of the plains, the eventual conquerors of Mycenae, Rome, and Kiev brooked no philosophical nonsense about the future. What they wanted they took and moved on. What they had they held, or perished. Likewise the peasant cultures, spread thin upon the land, looking from the earth to the sky and back to the earth again, heeded nothing of the future but the recurrent seasons, wished only to be left in peace, and wearied by toil had little urge to organize their affairs.

Not so the city-dweller. As Dr. Turner points out, one of the essential things about the city-dwellers is that they have a surplus. To obtain this required foresight; to retain it in the presence of many others, who were not of their kin or even of their tribe, meant the establishment of regulations controlling all predatory men, even themselves. This was the beginning of social control, of law and order as distinct from tribal military control; and as villages grew to cities, and their bounds became circumscribed because of the need of defense against marauders, the place where each lived had to be much more carefully defined than even the plots of the peasants in the crowded Nile valley. Each person had to have the right to get to and from his dwelling, and to the market place, and out of the city gates, and most of all to the well. Streets and public places, therefore, could not be encroached upon at the will of the individual, they were owned by all to be used by all.

This required organization and control. In some very ancient cities these had already reached a high point. In Mohenjo-daro in the valley of the Indus, for instance, which dates back to somewhere in the third millennium B.C. not only were the streets laid out regularly, but also different classes of society lived in houses of different heights, and the height of the houses determined the width of the street. A caste system of planning was thus established—not unlike the segregated planning of today, all the poor here, all the middle-class there, and all the rich elsewhere, with the Negroes and Mexicans nowhere. Mohenjo-daro also had a covered sewer system, the earliest known, which carried off waste from the private baths, which were part of almost every house. The connections were by chutes in the walls, carefully designed for the purpose and very similar to those in medieval castles. While not much is known, as yet, about this Indus River civilization,[2] there is no doubt that the social and sanitary services were highly organized. What is most striking, and as yet unexplained, is that there are no signs of organized religion, i.e. temples; and no signs of organized defense, i.e. city walls. These are the only known ancient cities without these dominations. They were mercantile cities which apparently perished, like the famous Cambodian city of Ankar-Vat, because the climate changed and the river deserted them.

We know that other very ancient cities were highly organized. Ur of the Chaldees, a city old in Abraham's time, was a place of perhaps a quarter of a million inhabitants. Tel-el-Amarna and Babylon were also great cities of many streets, requiring careful physical order and political control to make them habitable.

The plans of cities are enduring. Once the streets and other public places are determined, and the balance of the land is divided up into private ownership, nothing short of catastrophe or revolution will change the pattern radically—and not often even then. This persistence goes back far beyond Mohenjo-daro where the street pattern survived three successive re-buildings

[2] The river-flat culture of the Indus, of which Mohenjo-daro and Harappa are the (at present) outstanding examples, apparently deserves a place alongside the cultures of the Nile Valley and Mesopotamia. The results of the work of excavation (interrupted by the clouds of war) which was carried on under the direction of Sir John Marshall and his successors has been published in complete archeological detail and dryness. (*Mohenjo-daro and the Indus civilization.* Sir John Marshall, editor. Arthur Probsthain, London, 1931; and the work of Ernest J. Mackay, published in Delhi, 1937-38).

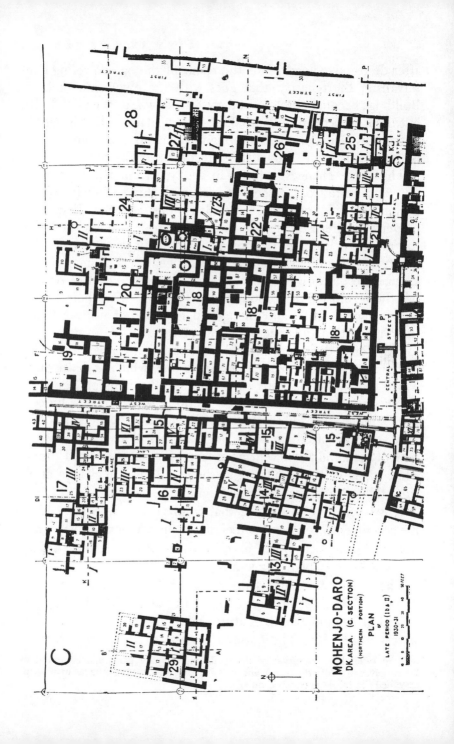

MOHENJO-DARO
DK.AREA. (G. SECTION)
(NORTHERN PORTION)
PLAN
OF
LATE PERIOD (ID & II)
1930-31

after destructive floods. It is the result of the overpowering conservatism, the tenacity, that goes with the ownership of land. Buildings become obsolete, and are torn down, or they fall down, but the land beneath remains. The "street that is called Straight" remains in Damascus, and although Caesar's palace is gone, tourists say with truth, "Down this street walked Caesar." [3]

Thus time changes nothing in a city, except the superficial, nor does catastrophe seem to change things much. Rome burned; so did London, so did Baltimore, and San Francisco. The fixed patterns of private property were too much for Nero; too much for the less tyrannical but equally powerless governments of the others. It is revolution that has done most to change the places where men live, not the revolution of politics but the revolution of economics and technics, with their accompanying social shifts and changes in methods of warfare. Even these revolutionary changes are most clearly visible in new cities founded after the event; the old cities show only a partial overlay of the new pattern upon the previous one, which is never quite wiped out. Medieval Paris sticks through the Paris of Napoleon III everywhere except in the new sections, such as Passy; indeed, the Gallic cross-roads that preceded even Lutetia persist today, only slightly shifted from the original lines. The same continuance of medieval and recent persists in every large city of Europe, while many of the smaller ones show little if any change at all from their Roman or medieval beginnings.

It is interesting to observe that from 3000 B.C. to the end of the seventeenth century, no technical improvements worth mentioning took place either in city planning or in those things which affect city planning vitally.

The open drains and semi-sewers of Mesopotamia were no different than those of most of the cities of the Middle Ages, or indeed of the nineteenth century. Washington, D.C., had open sewers until 1860. The covered sewers of Mohenjo-daro were

---

[3] An interesting discussion of this endurance of city plans can be found in Pierre Lavedan's *Introduction à une histoire de l'architecture urbaine* in a chapter called "la loi de persistance du plan."

smaller versions of the Cloaca Maxima; the latter differed not at all from the sewers of Paris, immortalized by Hugo. The walls of Troy and the walls of Verona differed as little as Helen and Juliet. The streets of Babylon and the streets of New Amsterdam were mud-paved, pig-scavenged, and lined with stuffy, badly heated, poorly ventilated brick houses. The aqueduct may once have been new, but even that is doubtful, for it derived from the irrigation ditch. In any case, few cities were supplied by them. Wells were the usual method of getting water, from the days of Rebecca the daughter of Bethuel to those of Rebecca Sharp.

Until the late eighteenth and early nineteenth century, indeed, the revolutionary changes were only two—although their impact was at varying times for various cities. The first one was the invention of gunpowder, before which fell the walls. The second was the change from feudalism to mercantilism, from the ritual of the church to the ritual of the court, from heaven to earth. The third, from earth to air, with who knows what social consequences to follow, we are going through today. For while the motor car gives increased mobility in two dimensions, the airplane adds a dimension. The first is merely an addition to an accustomed progression. The latter is new and revolutionary, physically, economically, and above all psychologically. The flyer returns to earth with an exaltation unknown to other men. Those who have heard the keen music of the black sky are never same again. We have begun to conquer three dimensional space, we are aware of four dimensional relations; in time we may conquer time.

All the ancient cities were surrounded by walls for defense.[4] The extent of the walls differed, depending on the type of site and the degree of power and wealth of the city, just as the material varied with the place, baked mud, fine brick, good stone, sometimes the palisaded fence. In hill-towns the hill-top was always the strong point, the sacred place. The lord spiritual or temporal lived there and the people clustered around his strong-hold. If

[4] As noted above, the Indus Valley cities seem to be an exception.

the city grew great and strong, the walls were enlarged: Athens, Rome, Toledo, are cases in point.

The Acropolis, once a fort, became the palace of Athena, the home of Theseus, the court of Justice. Below lived the people, guarded by a wall, outside were the fields and olive groves, Eleusis not far away, nor the sea which brought greater produce than the land—wheat from the Crimea, songs of Troy, knowledge from Egypt. Outside the walls, too, was the Academia, where winged words were spoken. So too Rome spread over the seven hills, walled; farmers, yokels, and the praetorian guard dwelt outside. The Romans were urban folk, and while the brief light lasted they wished to be within the walls where there was comfort in crowds; the dead dwelt along the Via Appia, outside. Sometimes cities grew outside the walls, overflowed down into the plain, and then the citizens took their chances when war came, or the "enceinte" was made large enough to take them in for protection.

The other type of walled city was the city of the river valley and the coastal plain, Babylon, Paris, the cities of the Low Countries. As these cities grew the walls were moved out, and often the old walls were razed and became wide avenues or parks which still exist. It must be remembered that none of these cities were very large, either in area or population, partly because they could not easily be defended if they covered too much ground, and partly because of the lack of technical means of providing for water, sanitation, and supplies.

On the hill or on the plain, dominated by church or by castle, the wall was the determining factor of the city plan. It made crowded living a necessity, except for a few of the rich and powerful. The restricted number of gates set the street pattern; this pattern was designed to make penetration difficult even if the gates were battered down. The streets were planned with off-sets, they were not intended to go directly from gate to gate or to the center of the city or the strong place. These things were not accidental, as Sitte [5] has conclusively shown. Often these

---

[5] Camillo Sitte, *Der Staedte Bau nach seinen Kuenstlerischen Grundsaetzen,*

irregularities led to space relations of charm and beauty. They invited three dimensional groupings of subtlety, sudden conclusions of form of great power.

The Propylaea gave grateful shade after the steep climb up the Acropolis, and the Attic sun lent decision and keenness to the eye as the alignments of columns shifted, and no building offered itself to view quite as the preceding one had done. The Greeks were too subtle to lend themselves to obvious symmetry. Only the Chinese were ever more subtle—and more inventive of form, more poignant, too. Peking is one of the great city plans, a unit of a manifold variety of parts, a pattern as intricate as the

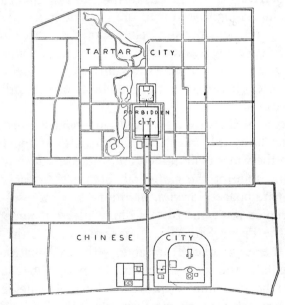

Peking: Plan of entire city showing main streets and axial approach. The plan shown on page 52 is of the Tartar City only.

Wien, 1901. The best of all the books on the art of town-planning, unfortunately never translated into English until this year when a translation by Lt. Charles T. Stewart will be published by Reinhold. There is a French translation, *L'art de Batir les Villes*. Another excellent work, based on Sitte's theories, is Pierre Lavedan's *Histoire de l'architecture urbaine*.

design of an ancient bronze, and as well ordered and composed. Peking was planned for Kubla Khan in the middle of the thirteenth century, and Marco Polo has left a highly ornate and vivid account of it, as strange and ornate as Coleridge's dream. He was enormously impressed, as well he might be, for in his day nothing like it existed in Europe. The basic order and good sense of its layout has persisted, although a good deal of the grandeur and orderliness has succumbed to time and war. Here is the superblock—the main thoroughfares making traffic-free islands of dwellings, infinite variety within a rectilinear frame. Here too is great monumentality—the long and splendid approach, through the gates of the Chinese city, flanked by the Temples of Heaven and Earth, to the gates of the Tartar City, and on in increasing splendor to the Forbidden City, the Palace of the Emperor, and the final climax of the great altar on the highest point. Peking was designed in three dimensions—the two storied palaces, the towers, the gates, all placed for definite effect, their gold tiles shining over the dull roofs of the ordinary one-story houses.

The medieval cities were full of drama—you stepped from the dark of the filthy side street, the houses almost touching overhead, into the wider main street, and there, ahead but not head on, was the spire of the cathedral; before you reached it, the market square opened for you, or around a corner was the guild hall. In Venice you came from a dingy alley out under an archway into the Piazza San Marco suddenly, or else the approach was from the sea, marked from afar by the exclamation-point of the Campanile, the great Byzantine gem of San Marco itself scarcely to be seen until approached by foot, shielded by the side-way approach through the Piazzetta, heralded by the Palace of the Doges. The eye never grows weary, the spirit never flags, as one walks in Perugia or Rothenberg, Salamanca, Salisbury, or Bourges; and this is not because of the architecture alone, but because the plan enhances the architecture, gives it scale and relationship, dramatizes it and places new values and new accents on it. There was always emphasis, focus, even in the meanest villages dominated by the meanest lords; Coucy stands like a thunder-cloud over the miserable huts at its base.

The little cities and villages of all Europe have their architectural gems; as Ralph Adams Cram observes:

> To build up a philosophy of Medieval art and a science of Gothic architecture on the foundations of only such structures as the abbeys of Caen, the Cathedrals of Chartres, Notre Dame, Rheims, Amiens, Beauvais, to the total ignoring of the work and the people as a whole, is absurd, for the art of Medievalism was essentially a communal art and to a degree never approached before. It was not the product of a few highly trained specialists expressing their own idiosyncrasies, but the spontaneous and instructive art of a whole people, or rather groups of people acting under a common impulse, in accordance with varying conditions, to a common end.[6]

This impulse, this instinct, included the city as a whole; as a communal expression the city was at least as important as the church, although the church pervaded when it did not dominate. It was not by accident that as society outgrew the central donjon and replaced it by the central church, that the church took the high place. Great care was taken that nothing should compete with it. The walls and towers of defense, the mansions of the rich, the lesser places of worship, the mass of houses, all were carefully subordinated to the climax. There were lesser emphases, digressions, intended to lead away so that the main theme would not be obvious or boring. If not wholly conscious the process of subordination was at least innate, a feeling for the fitness of things and their relationship in the life of the community that expressed itself as a just relationship in space. Al-

---

[6] Ralph Adams Cram, *Farm Houses, Manor Houses, Minor Chateaux, Small Churches in Normandy and Brittany*, The Architectural Book Publishing Co., 1917. See also the extraordinarily beautiful lithographs of French and Spanish cities and town, in many volumes generally titled *Voyages pittoresques et romantiques dans l'ancienne France*, published from 1820 to about 1860 under the supervision of I. J. Severin, Baron Taylor.

ways, in the medieval city, there were two compensations for the mud and filth, the danger and poverty, the ignorance and servitude: the overwhelming variety and beauty of Gothic architecture and the nearness of the open country.

Mastery of three-dimensional form, as well as the underlying two-dimensional pattern grew out of the technical factors of defensive purpose and the means of transportation. The defense was against men armed with man propelled weapons—bows and arrows, spears, battering-rams, siege towers, and so on, assisted to some extent by horses. Crooked streets, salients, sudden openings, made hand-to-hand street fighting difficult for the invaders who did not know the town. Transportation was almost exclusively on foot. Only those going on long journeys used horses or mules; intra-urban traffic was on foot even for the wealthy except on rare occasions of state. Carriages or other conveyances were all but unknown. When one is walking, architecture takes on meaning, it cannot be ignored. People become aware of form and relationship, consciously or sub-consciously, and this awareness has its effect on architecture and on city planning.

The medieval town was planned for the use of its inhabitants as individuals; and medieval architecture, for all its appeal to God and the hereafter, was a personal appeal, by men who made their contributions as individuals, and as individuals received their reward in the hereafter if not now. If the Cathedral meant all of the Summa to Thomas Aquinas, to the peasant coming in from the field it meant the stories of Christ he heard at his mother's knee, there visible on the voussoir. To the rising merchant class it meant honor and respectability, the gift of a window a finer record than a brass name-plate on a pew. Later on, after personal combat and the slow motion of the walker had given way to the impersonal cannonball and the swifter movement of the horse, this personality changed to an impersonality, a transfer of a feeling of oneness with God and a concern over his own chances for salvation to a feeling of mass unity in the abstract and a concern with the fate of the State as personalized in the King. Parades and power are not subtle; they need great spaces, and the obviousness of symmetry, together with simplicity, for gross comprehension.

The change of scale in the plan of the city and of the architecture, from Roman to Gothic and back to Renaissance also is an expression of this change. Gothic scale is small, carefully related to human size and custom. The cathedrals achieve their effect of grandeur by the multiplication of parts, within a carefully limited frame designed to lead the eye and mind on together, a suggestion always of more beyond. They are intended to be seen and appreciated part by part; even the interiors are multiple, and the only complete view is down the nave to the altar. As Sitte observes: "Since the exterior architecture of a cathedral serves only to express the interior form of the nave, it cannot stand being seen from far away in its entirety. Even on paper, in showing the side elevation of a church with its towers one must neglect the upper part of the spire if a well-ordered design is to be obtained. A complete geometrical view has not a satisfactory appearance. The Gothic cathedral therefore, benefits from being surrounded on three sides by narrow streets. It was enough that one wide street lead the processions and the crowds of faithful to the principal entrance." [7]

The Church is made for man, and this accords with the concept of man's importance in the eyes of God: the universe centers on man, whose soul is precious individually and specifically. Classical architecture uses the grand scale, in which the simple parts make up an undifferentiated whole, comprehensible at one glance. The effect of grandeur is achieved by a species of gigantism. Man is unimportant, the Gods or the State are outside of and unconcerned with the individual or his status. A similar difference is observable between Aquinas and Dante in contrast let us say, to Plato and Vergil. The Classic spirit is rational, reasoned, proportioned; the Gothic logical, mystical, distorted. Today, in our civic architecture, we have no scale at all, only great size quite meaningless either in itself or in relation

[7] Camillo Sitte, op. cit.

to anything else—it is neither rational nor logical, merely mechanical.

It was gunpowder—the ability to strike at a distance—that brought about the first major changes in city planning since the days of Jericho.

It happened, too, that the development of this mighty weapon aided and coincided with other changes, technological and sociological, of revolutionary importance.

J. D. Bernal, in *The Social Function of Science* [8] states this as follows:

> A new and important connection between science and war appeared at the breakdown of the Middle Ages with the introduction or discovery of gun-powder, itself a product of the half-technical, half-scientific study ,of salt mixtures. The introduction of gun-powder brought the striking repercussions in the art of war, and through it on the economic developments which tended to the break up of Feudalism. War became more expensive and needed far more technical skill, and both these needs played into the hands of the townsmen and Kings whom they supported against the nobles. . . .

> Gunpowder was to help science in many different ways. Not only did the need for the improvement in the quality of the powder, the make of guns, and the accuracy of fire, provide sustenance for chemists and mathematicians, but the problems they raised became the focal points of the developments of science. The chemical process of explosion led to inquiries into the nature of combustion and the properties of gases, upon which in the seventeenth and eighteenth centuries, the modern theories of chemistry were to be based. In their physical aspect the phenomena of explosion led to the study of expansion of gases and thus to the steam engine, though this was suggested even more directly by the idea of harnessing the terrific force that was seen to drive the ball out of the cannon to the less violent

[8] J. D. Bernal, *The Social Function of Science*, Macmillan 1939.

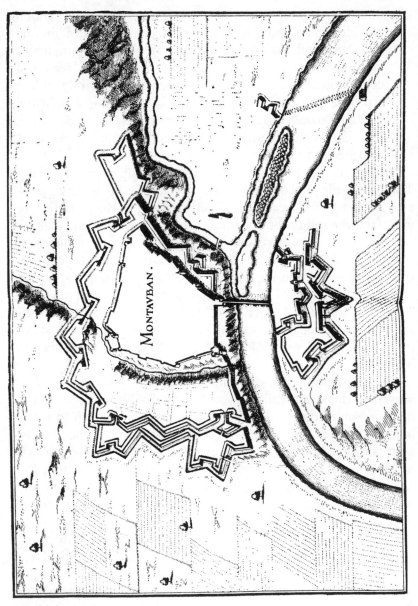

Plan of Montauban: This shows the development of city fortification from the walled hilltop to the outer ring of defenses.

function of doing useful civic work. The making of cannon provided an enormous stimulus to the metal and mining industries and led correspondingly to the development of inorganic chemistry and metallurgy. The great technical developments of South Germany and North Italy in the fifteenth century, where the basis of mechanical industry, capitalist economics and modern science are all to be found, were largely due to the concentrated war demand for guns and precious metals.

Artillery did not tumble down the walls at once, of course. The high walls of the feudal castle and the enclosed city gradually gave way to a new type of fortification, better designed to withstand the solid shot of cannon and the assault of men armed with muskets. They were lower, backed up by great mounds of earth—"defense in depth." These fortifications were no less constricting than the old high walls, but their planning required a new kind of engineering—in fact it was at this point that the "engineer" appears as a person other than the artist or architect, a man who specialized above all in the construction of massive structures for defense. Michael Angelo to Vauban, Vauban to Maginot.

At the same time, the economic and social developments were occurring that eventually brought considerable change to the interior plan of the cities. Mercantilism brought wealth to many more than ever before, and the humanist ideas of the Renaissance shifted the emphasis of spending away from the Church and the monastery to the luxuries of this world. Gold from the Americas increased the supply of money, and made possible the beginning of money-economy and the payment of wages in return for work or military service.

At this time, too, an Italian, one Luca Pacioli, invented double-entry bookkeeping—an invention much over-looked for its importance, and probably one aided in its birth by one of the many minor Devils. Werner Sombart (quoted by Harry Elmer Barnes in his *Intellectual and Cultural History of the Western World*) remarks all too succinctly: "Ideas of profit seeking and

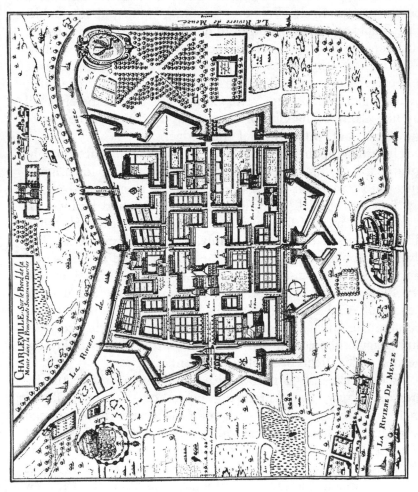

Plan of Charleville: A city of palaces, churches and convents—note the openness, the careful variety of axial treatment of approaches.

economic rationalism first became possible with the invention of double-entry bookkeeping. Through this system can be grasped but one thing—the increase in the amount of values considered purely quantitatively. Whoever becomes immersed in double-entry bookkeeping must forget all qualities of goods and services, abandon the limitations of the need-covering principle, and be filled with the single idea of a profit; he may not think of boots and cargoes, of meal and cotton, but only of amounts of values, increasing or diminishing." The Church wasted its time on small fry like Galileo. The City of God succumbed not to the law of gravitation but to the Rule of the Ledger.

The strengthening of the power of the central State brought greater security for trade and to the individual. The town house grew into a mansion with gardens, and the shop moved out of the house to specialized structures. Commerce and business expanded and men of like business needed to be near each other. The apprentice, one of the family, became many clerks. The dwelling could no longer serve the dual purpose of home and livelihood. The country estate came into being; the stern and repelling walls of Amboise and Chinon became the delicate beauty of Azay-le-Rideau and Chenonceaux, the Strozzi Palace became the Villa Medici. The wealthy took to using coaches; and heavy artillery mounted on wheels, with caissons following, needed wider streets and solid pavements.

Architecture had to follow with the changing times, the increasing luxury, the centralizing power of the State. Travel increased greatly, and the study of Classic and Roman design went hand in hand with the other arts and sciences. Not that the essentials of the old architecture were understood any more than Aristotle and Galen were understood; they served merely as a starting point for the contemporary expression of the new spirit. It was only when the humanist movement had passed into the neo-renaissance of the late eighteenth century that the architects and writers confused archeology and art.

The new avenues were lined with stately façades and pompous symmetrical edifices were erected on the great squares, the name

Gothic was invented in contempt of what had gone before. The avenues and palaces, the ducal mansions, the great estates and government buildings, the increasing wealth, luxury, and ease of life, left the living conditions of the underlying population unchanged unless for the worse. Behind the wide avenues, the medieval town persisted, unlighted, unpaved, unsewered, littered with garbage, ravaged by vermin and disease. The cities had grown beyond the walls, not yet interminably, but enough to lose

Karlsruhe: A princely city, focused on the palace.

much of the contact with the open country; and as population increased the denseness of buildings and the consequent squalor increased also. Moreover, the new wealth, together with the new enlightenment and culture, tended to concentrate in the royal cities and a few great trading centers. Paris, London, Amsterdam, Madrid, lesser places, such as Geneva, Lyons, Nancy, Karlsruhe, Berlin, St. Petersburg, drew all the rich, the powerful, and the ambitious. The "grand plan" developed, the axial composition, the broad sweep and the long, formal vista, the use of trees and lawns and fountains. The first great design was Michael Angelo's Campidoglio, a superb composition, followed by Domenico Fontana's new street system for Rome. The finest of all is the

Place Stanislas-Place de la Carrière in Nancy; the best known is, of course, Versailles, not the Palace alone, but the city. These and others are the basis of the "Beaux-Arts" school of city planning that reached unparalleled heights of perversion in the late nineteenth century. The masters of the Renaissance city plan understood as well as did the medieval planners the relation of buildings to street, the value of climax, the importance of the parts to the whole. The nineteenth century planners knew nothing of this: they said nothing, monumentally. They had as little regard for what went on behind the façade, where people lived, as *le Roi Soleil* himself, as though the two eighteenth century political revolutions had never occurred.

Far more important for the cities, although equally ignored by the architects who by now were leaving such things to the engineers, were the technological possibilities brought about by the Industrial Revolution. The thump and bang of early steam-engines at the mines, the new discoveries and theories in chemistry and metallurgy were to have far-reaching effects. Iron and clay pipe for sewers and water; gas for lighting; water-closets and bath-rooms; paved roads; railroads: the means of servicing great agglomerations of people. Advances in the field of health—antisepsis, control of dirt diseases, the discoveries of Lister, Pasteur, and Dr. Oliver Wendell Holmes. Mass production, the severing of the last links between home-production and the factory. The most extraordinary and unprecedented increase in population in the history of the world. The exploding shell replacing solid shot. . . . Imperialism, the concept of *laissez-faire*, the concept of democracy—the right of anyone to sleep under a bridge if he wishes to.

Paris set the new fashion for planning. Napoleon III, a fool and a despot, saw that the mob could not be controlled in the old city. Baron Haussmann, a despot but no fool, fixed that, not without profit to himself. Haussmann is the author of the Paris of the Boulevards as we have known it. He cut them ruthlessly through the old city, the most magnificent slum-clearance

job on record. He made them wide and straight, and he connected all the strategic spots, and provided circulation for troops
from any part of the city to any other, quickly and efficiently. It
made Paris what it is—or was—at a cost that must have made
Bismarck chuckle. No other major city in Europe was thus re-
modeled, and as the new Paris was at least shiny and new, and
with plenty of room for tourists who wanted their squalor and
dirt only as something picturesque, Haussmann was credited
with being a great city planner. Actually the great things of
Paris were all there before him—the ancient and aspiring power
of the Ile de la Cité, the vista of the Louvre-Etoile, the spacious-
ness of the Place de la Concorde, the Place Vendôme, the charm
of the Luxembourg, the Place des Vosges. The great "ring" boulevards had already been built by Colbert, on the site of the old
"boulevarts," or bulwarks. He had made a deal with the mer-
chants and landowners to finance this, and in return for their
aid he forbade any new construction of dwellings outside the
city. This smart deal resulted in the most unwholesome housing
conditions and together with Colbert's other innovation, the
"octroi" or customs-levy on all food and merchandise entering
the gates, did much to stimulate the disorders of 1789. Even in
Colbert's time—in fact since the days of Henry IV—Paris had
been too big and too unruly for its royal masters. Colbert's purpose, too, was to control the mob.

Haussmann added nothing, or nearly nothing, to that quint-
essential of city planning, the relationship of permanent things
in three dimensions. Streets and nothing else; two dimensional
ribbons for transit, and behind them the old city, paved now it
is true, lighted, sewered—but obsolete for living, largely a slum
since Colbert's time regardless of the medieval quaintness of
many of its parts.

The great cities of the Victorian age were planless, amorphous,
and horrible. Their rotted medieval cores were being surrounded
by workingmen's sections, row upon row of dull, dismal little
houses upon which the soot fell remorselessly.

New slums, modern slums, were growing up everywhere, faster

than Haussmann or Shaftesbury or anyone could cut through the old ones. The old ones were redeemed in part by the lasting vitality of their esthetic organization. They had been places in which people had once taken pride, which had been loved. The new ones had nothing. One slum was like another, block after block and mile after mile, unrelieved by a single accent unless it was the none-too-welcome one of a smoke-belching chimney. There was seemingly no end, for the dreary rows gave place to dreary "villas" which shredded out in the country without any demarkation. No one cared. No one could care. *Laissez-faire et laissez-aller.* Let George do it.

As to the older parts of these sodden towns, where the very poorest lived, or even where these miserable lived in the cities of the new world, the worst medieval conditions never equalled them for wretchedness. As has been said, the cities of the middle ages were small, the country was never far away, and if sanitary conditions were bad spiritual satisfactions were many. If there was not light, there was at least hope. The revolting conditions of the industrial slums have been often described: the reader seeking nausea may be interested in the contemporary accounts of Engels in *Conditions of the Working Class in England*, in the writings of Charles Dickens, particularly *Oliver Twist* and *Bleak House*, in Hugo's *Les Miserables*, and in the many official reports on New York quoted in James Ford's *Slums and Housing*. Or he can visit them for himself, today, for most of them are still there in all cities.

If the end of Victoria's reign and the false-quiet rule of Edward VII represented the nadir of urban living and urban planning, subordinating as they did every human quality in design to "amount of value considered quantitatively," there were counter-currents in preparation, subversive ideas, subversive—as they were to prove—techniques in the laboratory and in the mind: Robert Owen; Fourier; Karl Marx; Ruskin, the first to relate architecture and sociology (for the moral qualities Ruskin sought behind the stones of Venice are social values); Huxley, who saw as through a glass darkly that some day Science and

God must find a common meeting place in Man. An Englishman named Clerk-Maxwell, and an American named Gibbs, were to bring about the new revolution with "equations" more inscrutable, incomprehensible and powerful than the strangest writings of the astrologers and alchemists. They were not prophetic, for they were the future; they did not transmute iron into gold, they changed the face of the world.

It is time to look at our own picture, which differs somewhat from that of Europe.

2. PRECEDENTS

NONE OF THE CITIES OF AMERICA WERE MEDIEVAL, none were ever walled in, in the sense that Carcassonne was walled. From the beginning our cities were open cities, mercantile cities, free cities. Defense was only incidental, wooden palisades against the Indians.

For this reason the Colonial towns show a pattern quite different from anything to be found in Europe. It is true that New Amsterdam and Charleston showed vestigial traces of the European defense pattern, but Wall Street soon became a name and the bastions of Charleston didn't last long.

In the North, except for the coastal cities, the economy was primarily agricultural, the social life limited and simple. The emphasis was on a correct attitude towards God and a shrewd one towards your neighbor, the right to own land and to share in political activity and, gradually, to enrich life by education and the acquisition of goods from England and the Orient. The plans of all these cities centered around the Common; beyond that, old roads and topography influenced their layout most. There was obviously plenty of land, and the early settlers took ample lots and street widths. There were exceptions, of course, like Boston which if it was not laid out by cows certainly gave the impression that it was. As the cities grew, much of the original openness disappeared. The need to be near the center of the

city, at a time when only the rich had carriages and there was
no mass transportation, made useless the ample land beyond
walking distance. From time to time groups left and founded
other cities, but the ever-growing population continued to crowd
all cities more and more, and the sense of space, of free circulation of air and people was gradually lost.

Worcester, Mass., in 1839.

The small towns, particularly the "hill-towns" developed a
quite different esthetic, of which Litchfield, Ct., is a superb but
by no means isolated example. Litchfield was founded in 1720
as an off-shoot of Hartford. It was planned. There were sixty
parcels of fifteen acres each, and the purchasers drew lots for
their choice. The minister and the school master were assigned
twenty additional acres each. These splendid sites had an average
street frontage of about five hundred feet; the main streets were
three hundred and forty feet and two hundred and sixty-four
feet wide, with deep grass borders and elm trees on each side, a
stately setting. The houses, of course, were all one family homes,
starting modestly enough and growing into exquisite examples
of wood architecture.[1] Each house was a single thing, to be seen

[1] Although Litchfield was founded in 1720 most of the existing houses were
built a generation or more later, between 1750 and 1800.

as such, with its trees, its white fences, its garden. The fifteen acres were eventually subdivided, but Litchfield itself did not grow so large as to lose its sense of space. It is this conception of the individual house on its own lot, unrelated except in spirit to the neighbors, that is the essence of the American city plan, however perverted it became.

New Haven, a coastal town, was also planned. It was laid out as a square, diagonally to the harbor. The square was divided

Springfield, Mass., in 1839.

into nine blocks, the central one reserved for public use. Each of the nine squares was 858 feet on a side, so that here as in Litchfield, Milford, and elsewhere the "home lot" was ample for subsistence at least. As the town grew these lots were subdivided, and the squares themselves were split by new streets into four more squares, except for the central one which was split one way only—by Temple Street—and the one above that, also split only once, which was to become the site of Yale. This pattern remains today—Yale, the old churches, the Green, open and beautiful with the superb elms. The rest of the nine squares have gone the way of all such patterns, an indistinguishable mass of jammed together structures of all kinds.[2] "Greater New Haven," the city outside the Nine Squares, is no different than any other city of its time; except that the unplanned growth of Yale, filling in square after square with spacially unrelated buildings of the most absurd antiquarian pretentiousness, represents an opportunity thrown away.

In the South, things were somewhat different. Instead of a refugee, democratic, farming organization, it was aristocratic,

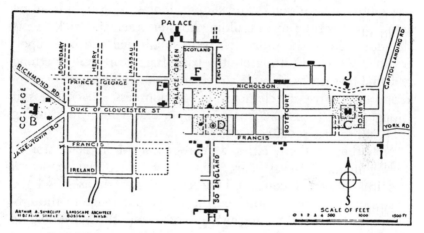

Plan of Williamsburg, Va. The Grand Plan scaled down to human living.

tenant, and plantation-owning. The focus was not on the town meeting and the church, but on the Governor and his little house of Lords, and the church was the Church of England. This difference is apparent in a different emphasis in the plan of cities. The New England planning derived not only from the character of its inhabitants, but from the character of the English villages and small towns, whence they came, with their informality and unpretentiousness. The southern tradition, in the main, derived from the tradition of the great baronial park and

[2] For a graphic representation of this process over the years see *An Atlas of Old New Haven, or the Nine Squares;* compiled by Dean B. Lyman, Jr., Chas. W. Scranton & Co., New Haven.

the formality associated with the aristocratic court. Williamsburg shows this clearly, with its fine axis closed by the Capitol at one end and the College of William and Mary at the other, its carefully placed Governor's Palace on a strong but minor axis, and the studied relation of the secondary streets and open spaces. It is a plan of exquisite relationships, a miniature, humanly scaled "grand plan." What happened to it between Colonial times and the recent restoration is an example of all that has been wrong with our civic development. The main street was cluttered with shacks and shops, filling stations and roadside stands, without regard to building lines or order; the back streets deteriorated and the properties were subdivided and built upon without control. Fortunately the basic framework was so strong and fine that it was possible to restore it, and although the restoration may have its elements of preciousness, nevertheless it brought back to us the finest example of small-town planning this country has produced.

No other southern cities were so excellent in plan, nor so wholly planned; nevertheless they show the formal tendency; and in the violent contrast between the great houses and the hovels of the poor is expressed the whole difference in the economic system of the mercantile North and the slave-holding South.

Savannah was an interesting variation. It was founded as "a practical philanthropy, a miltary necessity, and an agricultural experiment" by a group of colonists under the leadership of General Oglethrope. The plan was dictated by all three of these considerations. Mr. Francis Moore [3] writing in 1736 says:

> Each freeholder has a lot in the town sixty foot by ninety foot, besides which he has a lot beyond the common or five acres for a garden. Every ten houses makes a tithing, to every tithing there is a mile square, which is divided into twelve lots, besides roads; each freeholder of the tithing has a lot or farm of forty-five acres there and two lots reserved by the

[3] Quoted in *Historical Record of the City of Savannah*, by F. O. Lee and J. H. Agnew.

Trustees in order to defray the charges of the public. The
town is laid out for two hundred and forty freehold . . .
where the town land ends the villages begin; four villages
make a ward-out, which depends upon one of the wards
within the town. The use of this is, in case a war should
happen, the villages without may have places in the town
to bring their cattle and families in for refuge, and for that
purpose there is a square left in every ward big enough for
the outwards to encamp in.

Savannah thus started as a paternalistic democracy. The land
was entailed, no slaves were allowed, no distilled liquor permitted. This lasted only twenty-one years; for although it is hard
to assess the influence of the mint julep it is obvious that no
democratic, non-slave enclave could continue to exist in competition with the plantations of the Carolinas and Virginia. But
the mark of the planned community stayed—the regular order
of the streets, the lovely squares that were once camps of refuge.

The middle colonies have still another pattern. They were part
free-hold and part manorial, they stemmed from the Dutch, the
Quakers, and the Swedes. New Amsterdam was an unkempt,
planless village, for many years as constricted by the tip of the
island and the swampy land of the Lispenard meadows and the
Collect Pond as any medieval village by its walls. The history of
the New York City Plan is not colonial, and its pattern was set
by later influences, and will be discussed later. The upstate towns
were somewhat akin to the New England ones, but without the
forceful integrating influence of the Common and the town
meeting. Their economy was often more commercial, trading
posts, mining and smelting, glass and pottery, lumber. Their
plans were ample and pleasant, but lack focus. This is apparent
even today if one contrasts the over-all ugliness and squalor of
Albany with the greater variety and richness of Hartford, or the
peculiarly unpleasant character of Poughkeepsie with the charm
of Burlington, Vt. Even such open and generally satisfactory
towns as Olean, Ithaca, or Saratoga lack the feeling of civic unity

and organization that exist in, let us say, Pomfret, Ct., Hanover, N. H., or Manchester, Vt.

Philadelphia was another story. Penn was shrewd and sharp, and he saw in the broad reaches of the Delaware the great outlet of his principality. He (or rather his surveyor, Thomas Holme) laid out the city of Brotherly Love stretching from the Delaware to the Schuylkill in a hard rectangular pattern, the first of our gridiron cities, the first laid out with a cold eye for speculative profit.[4] The blocks were large, about 400 feet square, and the streets, with the exception of Market and Broad, were none too wide. The blocks proved unwieldy, there was too much inaccessible center land, and they were eventually split down the middle by alleys, which have been a detriment to the city ever since. The plan is quite unimaginative, but it was prophetic. Every block was just as good as any other, except, of course, for the commercial advantage of the Delaware frontage. The city was divided by Broad and Market, at right angles to each other, with a little park or "square" in each quadrant, and a good sized one at the intersection. The latter provided the only possible focal point anywhere, and so was sensibly chosen, eventually, for the site of the city hall. Philadelphia has, of course, more than justified Penn's foresight and faith in its industrial and commercial importance; it still suffers, as a place in which to live or work, from the aridity of his plan.

The outposts, the forts on the sites of Pittsburgh, Detroit, and Chicago, were abandoned as military posts before they had a chance to grow into fortified cities. Thus the typical American pattern was set from the beginning; the single family house, the individual plot of land, the expansible gridiron without boundary or form, directionless and exploitable.

Here comment must be made on what is the most famous of all our city plans, that of Washington, D. C., which, as everyone knows, was the creation of Major L'Enfant, with the assist-

---

[4] New Haven's Nine Squares antedated Philadelphia, but it was laid out for subsistence homesteads rather than as a city.

ance of one of the first great surveyors and speculators, Washington himself.[5]

Basically, the plan of Washington is alien to America. The idea of a new capital city was only agreed upon after Philadelphia and other places had been found politically unacceptable. Jefferson probably understood only too well how little either Philadelphia or New York had to offer in the way of satisfactory physical setting. Philadelphia today proves how right he was; and New York by the end of the Revolution was already sprouting germs of the 1811 plan in the 10th Ward—the present Lower East Side approximately—and in the suburb of Greenwich Village. Jefferson was enamoured of Paris—Paris, even then the city of regal vistas, the candles on the straight lines of chestnut trees lighting the way in spring for processions and stately equipages. He probably knew, too, that in the ancient side streets the mass of people lived in dank and festering squalor. For Jefferson the new capital of the New World was to be all avenues and vistas and no slums; for General Washington and the boys it was to be all profit. Neither expectation was fulfilled.

Considering that the site was a political compromise, that it was largely a malarial swamp, palmed off on the Federal government by astute speculators, L'Enfant's conception was truly magnificent and far seeing. How far seeing it was is clear when it is understood that for well over a hundred years it was not only unrealized but seemed unrealizable. Charles Dickens, Henry Adams, H. G. Wells have all written about the mud, the pigs, the ramshackle structures, the unfinished unsightliness of the town. For over a century Washington was a lot of muddy, unpaved streets; even Pennsylvania Avenue was sparsely lined by squalid shacks and dingy business buildings. The Mall was full of the Pennsylvania Railroad, the Capitol stood in splendid isolation on the Hill, and what there was of the city clustered around the Executive end of the town—the White House, State,

---

[5] For a discussion of the speculation in land that went along with the founding of the city by the Founding Fathers, see that very informative book, *The Great American Land Bubble*, by A. M. Sakolski. Harper's.

and Treasury—spreading out along Sixteenth Street, overflowing eventually into Massachusetts Avenue and along Rock Creek.

All this was contrary to L'Enfant's idea. He thought the Capitol would be the center, with natural residential growth on the high land. He faced the Capitol that way. But fancy speculation in land, together with the social pull of the Executive Mansion, turned the city around. It is only in recent years that the plan has been filled out in all its quadrants.

L'Enfant's original plan had many virtues some of which were modified in Ellicott's revision. Ellicott was a surveyor under L'Enfant, the "practical" man probably, and it is his version of the Plan, both published and executed, which is often confused with L'Enfant's. Aside from the famous diagonal avenue—rectilinear street pattern,[6] L'Enfant's great idea was the Capitol— Potomac axis, with the Executive Mansion on a shorter sub-axis at right angles to it, much like the plan of Williamsburg. Unlike the Williamsburg scheme, he further connected the Capitol and the Executive Mansion along the third side of the triangle by Pennsylvania Avenue. It was a grandiose plan, completely lacking in scale and impossible of visual success. Nevertheless, it was a unified conception until Andrew Jackson ruined it by placing the Treasury directly across the Avenue. This was the crowning point of the civic ignominy of the civically debased nineteenth century; at no other point in the history of urbanism could such a structure as the White House have been flanked by such things as Treasury and State.

A further defect of the plan was that it so completely ignored topography. Aside from the fine location of the Capitol itself, no consideration was given to the natural features of the site. This has resulted in some seriously unpleasant effects in the way houses are located in relation to street grade. Perhaps that is a minor criticism. The combination of a rectangular and diagonal street pattern has had the two-fold effect of making odd-shaped lots and of creating numerous traffic intersections,

[6] The first "diagonal" plan in this country, only partially realized, was Annapolis.

some of them developed as quite charming parks, but most of them are dangerous and difficult for traffic control, even with horse-drawn vehicles. Still more serious was the failure to develop any fine focus of national activity together with an appropriate architectural setting.

The lack of focus was not remedied by the famous Macmillan Commission, which, under Theodore Roosevelt, was given the task of rescuing the L'Enfant plan from the neglect and spoilation of the intervening years. It did do an essential and important job of getting the railroad out of the Mall, thus restoring some measure of integrity to that vast space, and re-drafting the plan to provide not only for the exigencies of the Union Station, but also working out new sites for public improvements, the Tidal Basin, the Memorial Bridge between Washington and Arlington, and other such monumental features. It failed, understandably, to overcome the essential lack of scale in the original plan; the Commission was to restore the plan, insofar as possible, not to make a new one. McKim, the architect who most perfectly expressed the spirit of the time, had little sense of site or grouping for architectural effect, he was immersed in the past and his scope was limited to the sympathetic reproduction of precedent. His restoration of the Washington plan therefore was unable to go beyond the original; fundamental mistakes were not rectified. The lining of buildings on each side of the Mall is ineffective; the width is too great. It is too long and cannot be held together, the way the Champs Elysèes is held together and terminated by the Arc de Triomphe at one end and the Louvre at the other; and it should not be forgotten that originally that vista was even shorter, for it was terminated by the Tuileries on the east side of the Place de la Concorde. The Washington Monument stands on high ground, which cuts the sweep of the vista except when looking down from the Capitol, and the paper relationships are never really realized; the Champs Elysèes is a long rise in one direction, the Mall is humped in the middle, like a camel. The Capitol, moreover, fails completely as a focus from any angle, and the other government buildings, the Senate and House offices, for which it is the dominating structure on paper are without relation to it in fact. The location of the Union Station, cock-eyed to the Capitol, is as inept an introduction to the city as could have been devised. The less said about the design of the station plaza, the better. The placing of the Library of Congress was not McKim's fault, but he need not have compounded the error by the site assigned to the Supreme Court. He was not, of course, responsible for either building. McKim, whatever his faults as a planner, had impeccable architectural taste. The proximity of these two architectural monstrosities to each other, however, takes the edge off of them, and they become ludicrous rather than ghastly. Downtown, the development of the Triangle, an inadequate space stuffed with pompous buildings by pompous architects, is neither functional nor monumental. From the civic art point of view it is simply terrible. There is no architectural emphasis nor architectural unity. The columnar treatment of the buildings is merely dull, and as each building is slightly different, the unity of Bath or the Rue de Rivoli is not achieved either. The enormous concentration of clerical workers in a small space without any provision for parking in proportion to their numbers, is inexcusable. Although the Macmillan Commission could not have foreseen this need, its plan could have been modified as the need became evident. It is not only in war time that Washington lacks organization, the lack is inherent in its diffuse and unfocused plan, the impossibility of making its two-dimensional grandeur apparent as three-dimensional reality.

Nor, to complete the tale of woe, is Washington without slums. It has, in fact, some of the worst slums in the country, some of them conveniently located in the very shadow of the Capitol. In 1940, twelve per cent of the dwellings in the District had no private toilet, five per cent had no indoor toilet, no electric light. This little history of the plan of Washington from the social rather than the monumental point of view is from the Housing Letter of the Washington Housing Association, Nov.-Dec., 1943.

WHAT HAPPENED IN WASHINGTON IN 150 YEARS

"The following history shows what can happen to a well-planned city when the plans are obstructed. Citizens see a problem, make protest, insist upon correction. Action is taken by the delegated authorities because of public protest, but suspended for one reason or another as soon as the clamor subsides.

1789—Washington, Jefferson and Major L'Enfant planned the Federal City. All buildings were to be constructed of brick not over 40 feet high nor less than 35. Squares were large. Lots were deep. Alley entrances were added. No wooden buildings were allowed.

1796—The prohibition against cheap wooden buildings was suspended until 1818.

1800—There were 109 brick buildings and 263 wooden structures, "small, miserable huts" people said. Many of them are still here in 1943.

1800 - 1860—Property owners built servants' quarters in the rear of their lots on the alleys.

1860 - 1870—Emancipated slaves 30,000-40,000 came to Washington. Some squatted on public land, constructing huts from refuse of military posts. Others constructed huts in the alleys. Kindly citizens seeing the insanitary conditions built brick houses in the alleys and rented them cheaply. They were popular with low income families. Private operators found it profitable to build in the alleys.

1870—Congress recognized the dangers of insanitation and established by law the D. C. Board of Health which attacked the alley problem by condemnation and demolition.

1870 - 1880—Alley dwellings continued to be built for profit. Social dangers of a large alley population continued to bring protests from citizens.

1892—Congress prohibits housing construction in alleys less than 30 feet wide and not provided with water and sewers, also in blind alleys which do not open to a street. The Commissioners were ordered to open, widen and straighten the alleys.

1894—The Commissioners were permitted to convert alleys into minor streets.

1897—Public spirited citizens formed a company to build limited dividend housing projects for families of low income.

1902—Another company was formed. The two companies gave up building in the expensive slum alleys in favor of construction on vacant land to reduce costs. Slum reclamation ceased.

1912—Congress appropriated $78,000 to clear and reclaim Willowtree Alley and convert the site into a playground.

1914—Congress forbade use of alley dwelling as such after July 1, 1918. Enforcement of the law was postponed because of wartime housing shortage.

1922—Congress amended the act permitting use of alley dwellings until June 1, 1923. An adverse court decision in 1927 destroyed the usefulness of the Act.

1926—The law for the condemnation of insanitary buildings was voided by an adverse court decision in favor of a slum landlord. Prior to this, about 5,500 had been condemned and 3,500 demolished.

1934—The Alley Dwelling Act was passed to provide for the reclamation of alley slums and the rehousing of the tenants. A revolving fund of $500,000 a year for ten years was expected to complete the work. The first year's appropriation was made as a loan from the Treasury. This was supplemented the second year by about half that amount from other funds allocated by the President.

1934 1938—Congress failed to appropriate the annual loan approved in the Act, Title I.

1938—Congress approved loans of one million dollars a year for five years but failed to appropriate the money.

1938—The act was amended to permit A.D.A. to borrow from the Federal Public Housing Authority under Title II of the Act.

1943—The Alley Dwelling Authority became the National
    Capital Housing Authority. The Authority now wishes to
    carry on its work of reclaiming the alley slums of Wash-
    ington and will soon present a bill to Congress for the
    purpose of continuing its work.

TODAY, after 150 years, 150 alley slums of 350 originally are
still here. They continue to blight both people and property.
The rebuilding of Washington is long overdue. The Federal
City can be the great metropolis of a new world planned by
Washington and Jefferson."

On the other hand, Washington's parks, its frequent open
spaces, its magnificent trees, go far to redeem the city, physically
if not functionally. There are spots of great charm and beauty
—the White House, Lafayette Square, the old City and District buildings on E Street, the wharves along the Potomac,
and of course Rock Creek Park. These things have human scale,
the eye can grasp them, the forms have some relation to each
other.[7]

The L'Enfant influence elsewhere was not great. He himself
was commissioned by Alexander Hamilton to lay out Paterson,
N. J., which was a pet project of Hamilton and his National
Association of Manufacturers. The plan proved "impractical"
and was not carried out. The "practical" boys and the "starry-
eyed" were at odds even then.

Two other cities started out with plans based on the L'Enfant
radial scheme. The Detroit "Governor's and Judges' Plan" carried the idea to its maximum logical possibility. It was one hundred per cent pure honeycomb, a resolutely hexagonal plan,
repeating itself endlessly over the endless flat lands. Fortunately
it was never carried out, except for vestigial traces in the downtown section, a confusion of angular avenues terminating

[7] For more complete study of L'Enfant's Washington, see Hegemann and
Peets *Civic Art*; magazine articles by Elbert H. Peets, and also studies by Alfred
Kastner and others, on the needs of the city today. An excellent brief summary
of the development of the plan of Washington, by Major General Ulysses S.
Grant 3rd, Chairman of the National Capital Park and Planning Commission
appeared in the *Journal of the American Institute of Architects* for March, 1944.

abruptly, after a few blocks, against the enclosing rectilinear streets. Buffalo, also, was supposed to be a radial city. One of the founding Ellicotts had worked with L'Enfant and in his plan for Buffalo attempted to adopt some of L'Enfant's ideas. His plan was not carried out except for four or five streets converging on the Square, forming part of the downtown city. Delaware, now the main avenue, runs into the Square in such a way

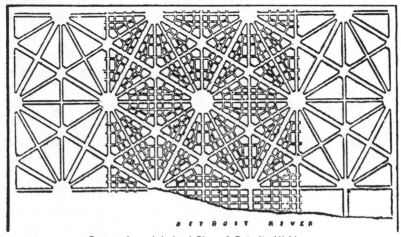

Governor's and Judges' Plan of Detroit, Michigan.

as to appear to miss it entirely, and what effect the new Municipal Building might have had in drawing it together as a focal point is spoiled by the unrelated mass and color of the Statler Hotel. An opportunity for a fine civic center 'was ruined by lack of control, in a place where control would be perfectly logical. Buffalo, like Chicago, failed to take advantage of the magnificent lake front. Chicago has been able to overcome this, at enormous expense it is true, and the great parks and drives along Lake Michigan are now among the finest in the world. Buffalo, however, resolutely turned its back on the lake, even the Municipal Building has its back turned to it. A visitor to Buffalo is not even conscious of its existence. Nor does Buffalo look down on the drama of heavy industry, like Pittsburgh with its apocalyptic views into the Monongahela Valley. Buffalo, like Detroit, is smoggy, flat, chaotic, and undistinguished, all its opportunities lost.

New York was one of the first great cities to follow the lead of Philadelphia and formally adopt the gridiron system. The famous official Plan of 1811 covered Manhattan as far north as 155th Street, and even that seemed daring and far-sighted, for

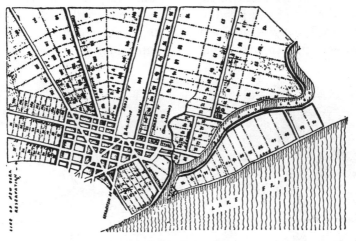

Ellicott's Plan of Buffalo.

New York was still a small city of less than 100,000 population —and Manhattan Island was still largely farms and country estates, with some separate villages such as Greenwich, Harlem, and Bloomingdale. But New York, although the phrase was yet to be coined, was aware of its manifest destiny. In 1807 Clinton's steamboat had voyaged to Albany, and in 1811, the year the Plan was made public, the Erie Canal was authorized. The future was secure. The plan was virtually an extension of the 10th Ward, the present Lower East Side, as can be seen from the Taylor-Roberts Plan of 1797. Manhattan was a variegated and beautiful island, much like parts of Westchester County, rocky, wooded, full of small streams, some of which ended in marshy inlets. It would have needed a good deal more vision and an entirely different attitude towards life to have taken full advantage of this in laying out the city, but even at that the Commission was a little extreme. Not a thought was given to topography or to existing roads—even the Bowery and the Bloomingdale Road (now Broadway) were to be wiped out. The scheme was substantially that which we know today. The principal changes have been the addition of Central Park, a revision of Washington, Madison, and Union Squares in minor respects, and the retention of parts of the Bowery and the Bloomingdale Road which were too powerful an influence to be overcome. The scheme provided uniformly saleable lots, and in terms of the day, pro-

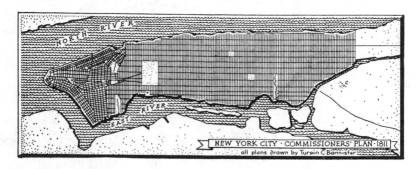

vided good circulation of traffic, which then was from river to river rather than up and down the island. It was a great improvement on the narrow streets of the old city below Canal Street from that point of view. Its failure is one of monotony, for no emphasis was possible anywhere, and as before noted, not even Central Park was provided for, but only five small parks and a Parade—again a reminiscence of Philadelphia.

The Commissioners actually stated that one of their objectives was a plan in which every site was equally good for any purpose, and their general point of view was expressed in the report,[8] part of which says:

> That one of the first objects which claimed their attention, was the form and manner in which the business should

---

[8] Commissioner's Report, 1811. Quoted in I. N. Phelps-Stokes' *Iconography of Manhattan Island.*

be conducted that is to say, whether they should confine themselves to rectilear and rectangular streets, or whether they should adopt some of those supposed improvements by circles, ovals, and stars, which certainly embellish a plan, whatever may be their effect as to convenience and utility. In considering that subject, they could not but bear in mind that a city is to be comprised principally of the habitation of men, and that straight sided and right angled houses are the most cheap to build, and the most convenient to live in. The effect of these plain and simple reflections was decisive.

*   *   *   *

It may, to many, be matter of surprise, that so few vacant spaces have been left, and those so small, for the benefit of fresh air, and consequent preservation of health. Certainly, if the City of New York were destined to stand on the side of a small stream, such as the Seine or the Thames, a great number of ample places might be needful; but those large arms of the sea which embrace Manhattan Island, render its situation, in regard to health and pleasure, as well as to the convenience of commerce, peculiarly felicitous; when, therefore, from the same causes, the price of land is so uncommonly great, it seemed proper to admit the principles of economy to greater influence than might, under circumstances of a different kind, have consisted with the dictates of prudence and the sense of duty.

No other street pattern than the rectangular gridiron could make headway against such dictates: ease of lay-out, ease of legal description, ease of merchandising. A lot could be sold from a map, site unseen. If it ran down a ravine or up a cliff or across a swamp, that was too bad: some day the hole could be filled in, the hill leveled, the swamp dried up, and then it would surely be the Most Prominent Address in the city!

What were so imperative and cogent reasons in determining the plans of Philadelphia and New York were even more compelling in places less felicitously situated. From the beginning of the settling of the continent the great colonial grants of land ran due west from the coast back into the unknown along the parallels of latitude. When lands west of the Appalachians were surveyed, they were laid out due east-west and south-north at mile and half-mile intervals. "Sections," "half-sections," and "quarter-sections" were the basis of all land dealings; quarter sections were the "homesteads" of the federal grants. When roads were put through they were laid along the mile and half-mile section lines. It was a simple system, and provided a simple base for city planning—often a necessary one, because the deeds already were written in conformity with it, and the legal framework, of course, could not be broken down. There were exceptions—central Detroit, as before noted; central Cleveland, Columbus with its capitol square recalling the pattern of the Colonial towns, and a good many other small towns which were founded in the early New England tradition—this is especially true in the Western Reserve, naturally. But these exceptions ceased with the westward march: Chicago, Denver, San Francisco, and all the hundreds of towns between, from Great Falls, Montana to Dallas, Texas, are nearly all repetitious of this same basic theme.

As a writer in the *American Builder* said in 1869, "In nothing is this uniformity more drearily oppressive than in the invariable rectangular arrangement of the country towns throughout the West. The traveler may journey for weeks upon the prairies, and visit hundreds of towns which, by the exercise of a little taste in adapting their arrangement to the natural features of their situations, might have assumed the character of charmingly attractive rural villages, but which are all so nearly repetitious of the same pattern that he can scarcely retain a distinctive recollection of a single one."

And earlier still, in 1830, someone wrote a series of articles entitled "Architecture in the United States" which appeared in the *American Journal of Science and Art* [9] for that year, in which

---

[9] *American Journal of Science and Art*, conducted by Benjamin Silliman, M.D., LL.D., January 1830.

city planning, civic art and architecture are discussed. Whoever wrote it was a keen and subtle critic, and well worth quoting from and reflecting on today, for what is well said is twice said:

In selecting ground for a town or city, regard should be had to convenience, beauty and health. The first of these is so chanceful in its character and so little subject to rule, that we must leave it to take care of itself which it will never fail to do; health and beauty are fair subjects for our consideration. The usual practice in our country, and particularly in the West, is to give even ground the preference, and when it cannot be obtained, the surface is generally levelled, often at considerable expense. . . . A city on level ground can never be a cleanly one. Extreme muddiness may be avoided by paving and extreme filth by frequent application of the scavenger's broom; after all this expense, however, such a place will be filled with offensive sights and smells. The offals of shops and kitchens will still accumulate; stables will send up their noisesome effluvia and mire will everywhere abound. There is no sweeping so good, while there is none half so cheap, as that which we may receive from a smart shower of rain. Such a cleaning however is impossible in a level town. . . .

Such a city can never be a handsome one. We may enrich it with marble palaces and deck them with ivory and gold, still it will be heavy and gloomy and dull. Everyone has read of Babylon, the city of sixty miles in circuit and one hundred brazen gates. It was the perfection of cities, if we make evenness of ground the standard; yet who that thinks of it, stretching league after league over the same unvaried plain, does not immediately tire of its uniformity. We turn from street to street, but the same dead level is before us. We look to the right and left, but the same prospect opens on either side; our feelings become stagnant and we can content to live there only by consenting to become as dull as it. Such is a level city. Let us now take a view of Rome. The simple word "in Capitolium *ascendit*" conveys to my mind, and doubtless conveyed to that of the ancient Romans, a more cheerful idea, than is suggested by all the wealth and pomp, and splendor of the proud drowsy city of the East. Rome draws half of its interest from its seven hills. . . . We may choose our ground well, but if it is not well used the choice looses half its worth. The ground too for many of our cities is already chosen and they cannot be removed; but they are extending their limits every year; New York, Philadelphia and Baltimore have doubled their circuit in the last twenty years; our other cities have increased theirs rapidly; Cincinnati has quadrupled hers in the last twelve or fifteen and so with many other of our western cities, and all this is still going on and will go on, for many years to come.

Our practice here too is beginning to set strongly toward one mode, that of squares or rectangular parellelograms. Philadelphia is laid out so, and it is a handsome city; Cincinnati is in the same fashion; I believe nearly all our western towns are so, and the custom is every year extending more and more. I am sorry to see it, and I hope the reader will be so too before we dismiss the subject. Experience shall be our guide in the discussion.

This is 1830.

All this lack of thought for amenity, this haste, this mechanical process of production, was unquestionably inevitable; disastrous things often are. There was not time for anything else, actually. No such expansion of urban centers had ever taken place before in all the world. They literally sprung up over night, and the settlers were none of them contemplative or modest. Each town was a future metropolis in their eyes, and their primary object was to make the town grow, to sell and buy and sell again. Land was not something to settle down on, it was a package. A town was not a place to live in, it was a place to make money in; even after it was a flourishing community there was little regard for what Ruggles called "the finer things of life." Moreover, there were no other city-planning concepts current or technicians other than the land surveyors; and the great plains forced no ingenuity upon them. It was doubtful if they had the ingenuity to develop anything else, even if they had the time. For the gridiron rides rough shod over the steep hills of San Francisco, just as the straight furrow rode rough-shod over hill and dale regardless of contours, regardless of the rains that washed the earth away.[10]

The development of cities during the great era of expansion was determined by the social content of the time. They were planned physically for the primary purpose of land speculation; there was no planning for living, for economic growth, or for social benefits because these things were uncomprehended. The early Colonial towns were the result of specific American circumstances and a seventeenth and eighteenth century European background and culture, especially English, with Continental overtones. By the time the course of empire was taking its way westward, this tradition was already lost, except along the narrow fringe of the Atlantic seaboard. Even there it remained only as tradition and not as living force. Later it was to return as something nostalgic and desired, longed for but spurned as something foreign and unworthy of a nation of Pioneers and Builders. If the first settlers of the mid-west and western towns were forced into rigid patterns by the iron of material and mental poverty, their successors of the post Civil War period were equally driven by the forces of a different metal—gold, and the doctrine of the new Puritanism that the only thing in life was work, and the only reward was the acquisition of wealth. It was the period that drove Clemens and Blakelock to despair, Henry James and Whistler to

[10] It is interesting to note that the great engraved plan-and-view books of the seventeenth century distinctly show the practice of contour-planning in the fields surrounding the hill-towns. See the work of Zeiller-Merian and particularly Jon Blaeu's magnificent work *Tooneel der heerschappyes van zyne koninglyke hoogheyd den hartog van savoye* published in 1697.

These and other engravings of seventeenth century cities were the direct result of the new developments in warfare. They are works of espionage, supplying information on fortifications, and in the case of Zeiller covering all of Europe with German thoroughness. That they are also works of art is quite incidental. Whistler, it may be recalled, was fired for trying to put the same quality into the Geodetic Survey.

England and unknown others into silence. No such flight was possible for the city.

So within the framework of the gridiron patterns of living were set up. Main Street appeared—the wide road, with the false front business buildings, porticoed for shade and with hitching posts for the convenience of patrons. The residential streets, too, were wide, but not paved for their full width, there were grass side strips and trees, and the houses were set well back as in the Colonial towns. These were single family houses, the front lawns

Lowell, Mass., in 1839. Factories on the flood plain.

merging into one, the back yards, with the stable and privy, decently fenced. As the city grew, the pattern did not change, it was only intensified. The business section spread, the buildings became four and five stories high, of substantial brick. The inner residential streets developed narrower lots and smaller houses, finally to become solid rows, the back yards now closed in by high board fences. The wealthier citizens moved out, onto larger lots, their houses became more ostentatious, sprouted gables and turrets and towers; the estates of the very wealthy were surrounded by wrought-iron fences because stone walls were considered undemocratic, and besides the iron fence permitted admiration and envy even as a barrier. Sewer systems and central heating came, and "macadam" roads and the Welsbach light. The railroad came, and factories. "The wrong side of the tracks" sprang up, mean shacks and shanties.

Property rights were a sacred thing. "Nobody can tell me what to do with my land." The locations of factories and warehouses were determined only by the cheapness of land—usually river bottom land, along marshy creeks, or other places where industrial wastes could be dumped, sidings run in, and immigrant tenement houses thrown up. The ultimate destination of the polluted water course did not matter, the desecration of lake fronts, such as that of Chicago, did not matter. The flooding of the low-lands, Pittsburgh, Cincinnati, Lowell, did not matter. The health and ultimate fate of the wops, hunkies, greasers, or of their children, did not matter. Railroads, penetrating the heart of the cities, filled enormous areas with freight and switchyards, the steam locomotives were as thunderous and smoky as a steel mill. The downtown areas grew higher, the buildings crowded closer and closer together. Apartment buildings replaced the row houses; street cars brought more land into reach, and sub-centers began to grow up. The towns became cities, and the cities reached out and swallowed the towns. Municipal services grew; the problem of sewage became ever more acute, disposal plants had to be built. So did garbage disposal plants, for the garbage dumps, once on the edge of the town, were now in the city. Water supplies became polluted beyond the point of safety, so new ones had to be found, purification plants had to be constructed, or the water brought from far away. There were new demands for street lighting, street cleaning, paving, libraries, parks, better schools; the demands on police and fire departments increased; hospitals, jails, welfare agencies and new municipal buildings were needed.

It was an expanding economy. Cities doubled, trebled in size in the decade between census takings. Everyone knew when the corner of Tenth and Elm was "way uptown." Everyone had an uncle or a cousin thrice removed who had once owned where the First National Bank now stood and had sold it "just too soon."

In Chicago the floor of the Palmer House bar was paved with silver dollars, on which stood brass spittoons.

The excessively rich sought vindication by magnificent gifts of land for parks, for institutions of all kinds. They went abroad and brought back memories of the magic of the boulevards of Paris, of Hyde Park, of Unter den Linden, of Italian Palazzi. In spite of themselves they had been impressed, not as Henry Adams had been impressed by the mystery or introspective beauty of Gothic, but by the power and blatancy of the Column and the Dome. They sought to emulate, to express their own power in magnificent civic works in cities devoid of every element of civic art. Corrupt government as well as corrupt wealth contributed—many of our finest civic improvements are directly due to crooked politicians who found in great public works their richest source of graft.

The flood of immigrants spread into the older residential districts from the river-bottoms, congestion and poverty increased with economic feudalism and wealth. Great town houses were built, and blocks of tenements. The hitching posts had gone, and the trees; buildings edged out to the paved sidewalks.

The end of the century saw the American city at full tide. The recurring "business cycles" still went up more than they went down, and little cognizance was taken of the decreased rate of increase. It was assumed that the value of land would always increase faster than the "improvements" depreciated. Popular psychology became more and more fascinated with the notion that "money works for you," and if you are smart enough, you don't have to. One consequence of this was a change in the attitude towards mortgages. Money invested in homes was considered "tied-up"—mortgage your house and let the money work. The old sound, conservative idea that a mortgaged home was a disgrace was replaced by the smart idea that not to have a mortgage was evidence of lack of enterprise.

The development of the steel-framed skyscraper also affected the city. It made unheard of congestion possible and ran up property values, because of the enormous increase in rental area which was made available. It also was a new cause for civic pride, and many a small town built at least one unnecessary tall building for that reason only. Horizontally, the horse-car had been superseded by the cable-car, and that in turn by the trolley car. Electric lights and power were coming along. Marconi was finding practical application for Hertz' discovery. The Age of Electricity was at hand, and the automobile.

It was the automobile that really broke down the city limits. The wealthy promptly moved out. The great houses "in town" became empty. This movement was emphasized by two things; the motor car which on the one hand filled the streets with noise and fumes, and on the other provided the means of escape; the restriction on immigration which created a "servant problem," both by stopping the influx of the "servant class" and by making better employment opportunities in industry. This affected the upper middle class particularly, and they built more compact and convenient houses in the suburbs, where they demanded—and got—new schools and generally better living facilities for their taxes. The old mansions stood empty and deteriorated, or were sold for rooming houses. Filling stations, dog wagons, parking lots, filled up the spaces between, along what had once been fine residential avenues.

Down-town, the electric elevator had created the super skyscraper, and the tall structures rendered the old business blocks obsolete. The streets were jammed with cars—villagers and farmers for miles around came to swell the crowd. The modern hitching post, the parking meter, appeared. The electric sign did its share to ruin the city, for the little stores and sub-centers in the residential areas lighted up too, and became foci of distraction and irritation. Enormous costs were incurred for repaving, street widening, and the creation of plazas and parking areas. Equally enormous costs went into national highways, all of which formed a subsidy to the automobile manufacturers while emptying the cities of their best tax payers. The electrification of railroads helped the spread of population around many large urban centers. The indirect costs of traffic congestion began to be apparent,

and factories began to move out. Business, too, saw the hand
writing on the wall—it built branches in the suburbs, or on the
edge of town with ample room for parking.

All this meant loss of revenue to the municipalities. Their tax
rates were usually limited by law, their bonded debt was usually
excessive, and they could not cut their operating expenses much.
People had become accustomed to services, and the payrolls were
fixed by political indebtedness and the demands of intrenched
civil servants. The multiplication of the governmental entities
was a burden too, they overlapped, they duplicated, they were
vestigial remains persisting solely because of payrolls. Cities were
divided into wards, precincts, health districts, census tracts,
school districts, overlaid with Townships, Counties, and special
fiscal areas for water taxes, sewage taxes, park assessments, shot
through with ancient franchises, utility monopolies, burdened
with hundreds of vacant lots in half developed sub-divisions, obsolete business structures, blight, and slums.

This is their condition today. They survive because a city is
people, and people like to live in them, and the process of break-
ing down takes a long time. In fact, they cannot break down
completely. Before that happens the people who make the city
will change the patterns, physical, economic, and political, to
ones that will survive.

Main street, Mohenjo-daro: A view of a small portion of the excavations.

Plan of Peking. "Plan de la ville Tartare." "A pattern as intricate as the design of an ancient bronze."

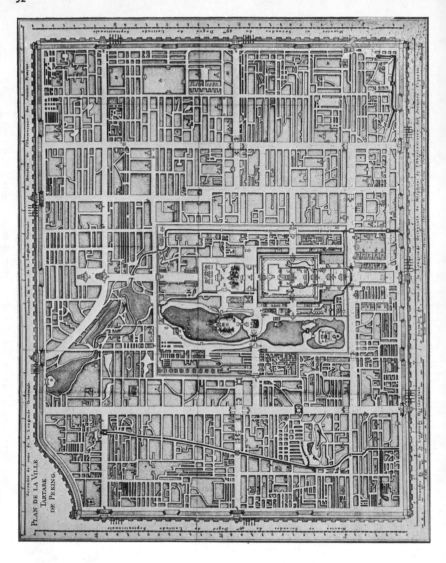

Butstadt: The city as a market place, 1639.

Brighton, Massachusetts. The city as a market place, 1839.

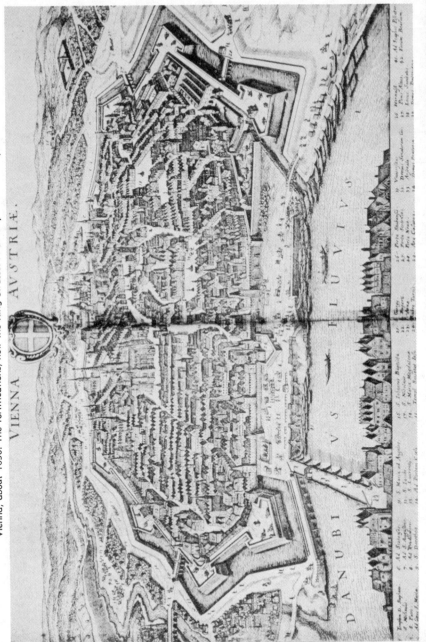

Vienna, about 1630. The fortifications, now the Ring Strasse. A densely croweded city even then.

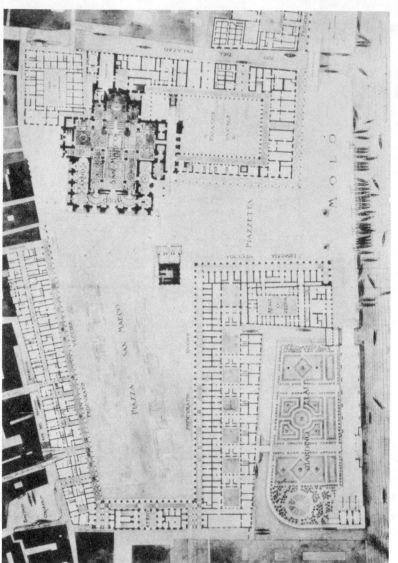

Piazza San Marco, Venice. Note the careful displacement off-center of axes. The domes of St. Mark's and the Campanile dominate from the sea, they need not dominate from near, but can take their place as part of the total composition from within the Piazza. Note too how the Piazzetta widens, and how the projecting Logetta instead of constricting the approach lends interest to it and acts as a foil to the Byzantine splendor of the church.

The Capitol, Rome. "Il Campidoglio"—a Michael Angelo masterpiece of planning. More direct in its attack than the Piazza San Marco in Venice, it makes full use of the drama of its topography, and of the relation of adjacent buildings and approaches.

Piazza Navona, Rome: The Renaissance plaza. The church and obelisk are not on axis with the street opposite; the plaza itself is a recess off the streets entering the two ends. The turbulent magnificence of the Baroque architecture is one with the turbulence and activity that goes on in the plaza.

Château de Villandry, France. "The stern and repelling walls . . . became delicate beauty."

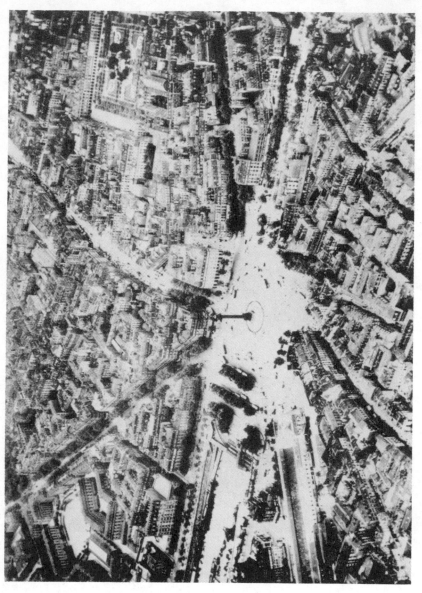

Haussmannized Paris. The Place de la Bastille. The lines of new boulevards show clearly; the ancient congestion behind them shows equally clearly. Top right, the Place des Vosges.

Litchfield, Connecticut. The splendid setting . . .

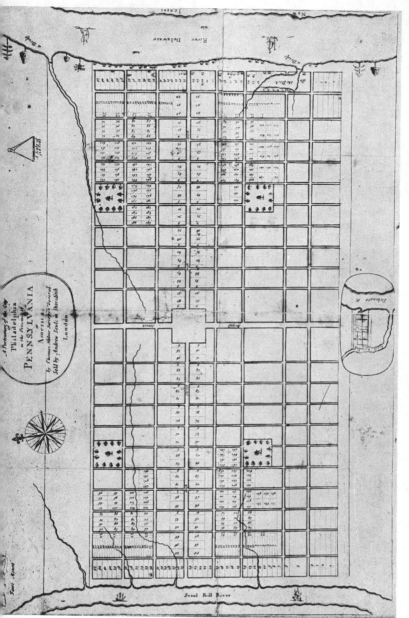

Plan of Philadelphia. The Holme plan of 1683. Showing the four parks and the common (now occupied by the City Hall). The blocks have since been divided by alleys. This is the pattern that makes downtown Philadelphia what it is today.

Brockett Map of 1641

Doolittle Map of 1812

Airplane Map of 1929

Three plans of developing New Haven, from the original plan to the present day.

Washington, D. C., 1800. The Ellicott version of the L'Enfant plan. Monumental but unclear. The scale is enormous, and the supposed relationships cannot be felt on the ground.

64

Utica, 1807. "Group" houses as well as single houses; unpaved streets; no focus or order. Unlike many cities of the period, the houses are small and mean, and are set on the building line. Note the town pump.

Utica, New York, about 1850. The cities were expanding.

Oklahoma City in 1890. "A City of 10 Months." The apotheosis of the gridiron.

3. APPROACH

> In the main, until the rise of machine production and industrial cities, all social and cultural developments were merely superimposed upon peasants and nomads, who had lived, worked, behaved, and died in the manner of their ancestors, generations without end. Upon the continued performance of routines of life in neolithic achievements, rested the order, stability, and wealth of all subsequent cultures. In those routines was taken up that burden of labor in the fields, on the plains, and at the simple crafts which was to be the lot of common man until very recent times. Even in the most advanced industrial nations, it should be recognized the masses of the population are only a few generations away from the organization of life that came into existence at least seven thousand years ago.
>
> —Turner, The Great Cultural Traditions.

AS WE HAVE SEEN, CITY PLANNING IS NOT A NEW THING in the history of cities, nor is it a new thing in this country. The expressed purposes and attitudes of city planning in the past fifty years are perhaps different from those of earlier times, and it will be well to examine briefly both the attitude of planners and that of the public towards planning.

The realization that our cities were inadequate and needed replanning came forcibly into public consciousness with the revived public awareness of architecture which began with the Chicago World's Fair in 1892. This story has been told again and again. The White City brought into focus other values than those of the market place, showed for the first time ordered classic beauty on a great scale. It was designed by men brought up in the tradition of the Ecole des Beaux-Arts, who had lived in and loved haussmannized Paris. Chicago, at that time, was a blot on the face of the earth, Washington was a mess of muddy streets with the Pennsylvania Railroad running through the Mall, New York, Philadelphia, St. Louis, and all the rest were raw, unkempt, and disorderly. The men of the Fair had a vision of ordered symmetrical beauty, of shining buildings in orderly array, the vast distances of Versailles, the Place de la Concorde in the blue Parisian haze, the pride of Roman fora with silk-hatted Senators bowing before Mark Hanna. They felt that here was the fitting and proper form for America, America which was in full tide of recovery from the disasters of the '70's, America, whose manifest destiny was at last becoming visible to all the world. The Industrial Age was at its peak, the doctrine of *laissez-faire* was undisputed except by a few crack-pots, "socialists," people who read Marx or remembered Horace Greeley, political agitators like Debs and Altgeld, a lunatic fringe of malcontents, people who confused Kropotkin and Bakunin. There was also Louis Henri Sullivan, architect and seer, who knew a hawk from a handsaw, and not only when the wind was easterly, a prophet of the shape of things to come, the architectural counterpart of Thorstein Veblen. The Corinthian Order of Imperial Rome was the order of the era. From the boards of platitudinous architects it emerged as a vulgarization of the vulgar, a stereotyped manifestation of economic authoritarianism. The Roman fasces became Americanized: $.

Nevertheless, civic thinking had to start somewhere, and if the point of departure was the Court of Honor and the culmination was Burnham's plan of Chicago, still it was planning, and the idea spread through the land. Cities started to wash their faces even if their underwear was still dirty.

Civic pride naturally took the form of public works, and the city plan generally meant the paper architectural development of a civic center, often with approach streets widened and lined with uniform greystone buildings in the best Rue Castiglione manner. The focal building always had a dome; its portico had a pediment, and the pediment was full of bank presidents, disguised as Greeks, hammering golden spikes into transcontinental rails. There were fountains, and trees *en espalier*, and the pavements were marked off in marble blocks. Tripods held up by griffins provided light, and the Horses of Marly threatened passers-by from all angles. Fortunately, little of it came to pass, except in Washington and an occasional place that got out of control, like Harrisburg.

How little anything except stereotyped formalism meant to the architects of that period is best demonstrated by what McKim did to the campus of the University of Virginia, Jefferson's love and monument. The architecture is early "Greek revival," Jefferson's own strangely transmuted and lovely version. The library is on the high point of the hill-side, the residence buildings step down two sides of the tree-studded slope, variegated, charming, informal, and dignified. Out beyond, the view spreads across the valley to the hills in the distance. It was one of the best examples of site planning and architecture in the country. When the University needed some new buildings, McKim placed one of them, a dull thing too, directly across the open end of the axis.

This obsession with the formal and the moumental, "the grand plan," was quite in accord with the spirit of the times, just as it was in the days of the Roman Empire and of Louis XIV. Analogies can be pushed too far, but there is a relation between the Baths of Caracalla and the Roman slums, Versailles and the stench of Paris, the Pennsylvania Railroad Station and the Lower East Side.

In the meantime, while the Corinthian Column was thus marching on, the Garden City movement was reviving in England, where Ebenezer Howard's ideas brought new life and meaning to the human planning which had commenced with Robert Owen and gone into eclipse with the triumph of Manchester and the failure of New Harmony, Ind., a socialist co-operative venture founded by Owen in 1825. Owen, a most extraordinary man, was an industrialist and idealist who was shocked beyond reason by what the new industrialism was doing to the Midlands. He came to this country to try to put his Socialism into practical form. His was among the first of many cockeyed experiments, most of them interesting sociologically, but without much repercussion on city planning, although Owen had prepared diagrammatic plans for an ideal working man's town that was remarkably far sighted and well-ordered in its functional arrangement. New Harmony was originally a town on the Wabash founded by a celibate sect known as Rappites, Pennsylvania Germans who had trekked through the wilderness in 1814 to establish the town of Harmonie and live out their lives in isolation. Owen bought them out, and they went back to Pennsylvania, called their new town Economy, and eventually disappeared through the natural process of celibacy. They were an unattractive crew. Owen purchased the town and thirty thousand acres of land, renamed it New Harmony. As a co-operative venture it failed after two difficult, stormy years, but it continued for many more as a normally constituted community of unusual progressiveness in social methods, and as a remarkable intellectual center, under the leadership of Owen's son, Robert Dale Owen. It is today a quiet Indiana town.

Owen's contribution thus was more in the field of social theory than in town planning. The effect of his ideas was not directly on physical aspects, but on the control and use of land for the benefit of the workers, and on the concept of the integrated community. He realized more than his predecessors, and most of his successors, the importance of combining work-location and living, education and practice, economics and politics.

This whole pre-civil war period was marked by cultist reactions to the prevailing materialism, crassness, and dog-eat-dog attitude. New Harmony had its neighbors in the wilderness, long since forgotten; while in the east there were the Fourierist "phalansteries" approved by Emerson and the rest; there was the Oneida colony, the most successful of all except perhaps the Mormon towns in Utah. And, of course, there was the famous one-man Exhibit A, Henry Thoreau himself. Then in 1851 a man named John Stevens organized a series of "Industrial Homes Associations" to provide homes co-operatively owned in the environs of New York, in an effort to escape the tyranny of the landlord. The promotion literature reads like a mixture of Engels and Henry George, badly digested. His efforts were backed by Horace Greeley—who ran articles by Karl Marx in the *Tribune* and was otherwise queer. There were three of these Associations formed, Number Two surviving as the City of Mount Vernon, New York. The Association itself failed of its purpose, as did all the others except Oneida and the Mormons—the only two which fully realized that co-operation must rest on a firm economic base and common social interests and not just on casual association for the purpose of land-ownership. None of them allowed sufficiently for the unstability of human affairs. As the historian of Mount Vernon, John G. Wintjen, succinctly says, "It was not long, however, before some exchange of property took place [land was originally chosen by lot] among the early members of the Association while others, unable to continue their payments, were obliged to dispose of their holdings or turn them back to the organization for resale." So many of the original members moved away, and strangers who were not sympathetic to the purposes of the colony came in. Even reversionary clauses in the deeds were only effective temporarily. The pressure for speculative profits and expansion was too great to be resisted, or if resisted, it drove the enterprising elsewhere. Yet the basic idea of land controlled by all the citizens of a town, with the incremental increases in values accruing to all, is a perennial one. Ebenezer Howard revived it, and the Greenbelt Towns of yesterday and the "Mutual Ownership" developments of today—of which more later—are attempts to do the same thing.

Ebenezer Howard was a London clerk, who, like Owen, was appalled by the horrors of the industrial slums. He wrote a book, first published under the title *Tomorrow*, later called *Garden*

Cities of Tomorrow, in which he advocated, in detail, most of the things that are the commonplace of small-town planning today. He became a crusader for his Utopia, which differed from the Utopias of the social revolutionists in that it offered a definite plan for accomplishment. He took the idea of an industrial dwelling town and set it in an agricultural belt. The size of the town was pre-determined, and its plan was based on convenient use, an integrated pattern of industry, commerce and living. As needed, other "satellite" towns were to be built, for the "greenbelt" was never to be encroached upon, nor the industrial town allowed to attain excessive size or density. The greenbelt was to be more than a protection; Howard intended it to be definitely agricultural and a source of food supply to the town. "Farm belt" would perhaps be a better term for his idea. Each town was to be connected with others and with the central metropolis by a system of inter-urban railroads (he wrote before the automobile and the super-highway). The land was owned by the Corporation, but the inhabitants controlled the government. Unlike Port Sunlight and other "model towns" erected by industrial concerns as profitable philanthropies to ensure contented workers—Shaw has brilliantly etched one of them in *Major Barbara,* seeing clearly, as usual, through the pretense and the sham—these were not to be "company towns."

Howard's principles had a profound influence on planners everywhere, and on promoters too. In England it resulted in two cities—Letchworth, planned by Raymond Unwin, and Welwyn, planned by Louis de Soissons. These two towns have been successful, in the main, although neither of them has grown to their full pre-planned size, nor have they attracted as much industry as hoped for. Many of the ideas developed and expanded by Unwin were basic to the various "estates" which were built in England by both public and private enterprise. These ideas also greatly influenced German planning, and the work of Ernst May, Walter Gropius, the brothers Taut and others. Unwin, who spent many of the latter years of his life in this country, also exerted very great influence on our own concepts, through his teaching at Columbia University, lecturing, and discussions with technicians and administrators in the early days of public housing. He wrote books and many articles;[1] his pamphlet, "Nothing Gained by Overcrowding" is the basic statement of the problem of density of land use, and was instrumental in establishing the generally accepted English standard of twelve families per acre for all new (non-metropolitan) developments.

All these various efforts at land control were within the framework of *laissez-faire*, i.e., they were brought about not by legislative invasion of the right of the property owner to the land beneath and the air above, but by the mutual agreement of private groups, whether "co-operatives" as in the case of Mount Vernon or joint stock companies as in the case of Letchworth. The control of land was voluntary control by the owners, not imposed by society through government.

This does not mean that there were no legislative bars to public nuisances and health menaces, which of course are very ancient. New York City early in its career regulated the location of glue factories and tan-yards for instance, but these and similar regulations were against obvious and limited nuisances. Building laws gave a measure of structural safety and fire protection. Thus over the course of years a firm legal foundation was established for the control of building under the "police power" of the state in the interest of public health, safety, and the common welfare. It was as a part of this conception of public welfare that in 1916 the first *general* land control law in this country was enacted. This was the "Building Zone Resolution" in New York City, controlling the use of land and the size of buildings as part of the police power. Like all such enactments, it was the result of a long series of abuses which had finally reached the point of menacing the interests of large land owners and so permitted action.

Unrestricted building on lower Manhattan had attained fan-

[1] His principal work *Town Planning in Practice*, is a standard reference book.

tastic proportions, for the steel frame and the electric elevator made anything possible. What finally forced even the real estate interests to a realization of what it all meant was the construction of the Equitable Building, 120 Broadway, thirty-eight stories running solidly from Broadway to Nassau Street, casting a shadow covering over seven acres on bright winter days. Broadway is only 80 feet wide there, Nassau 45 feet, and the north and south bounding streets, Cedar and Pine, only 35 feet each. It became quite clear that unless controls were set up all downtown property would be ruined. There were also signs of rapidly increasing deterioration in residential sections because of the intrusion of business or manufacturing, and of apartments into single family areas.

The first zoning law, which applied to New York City alone, faced all kinds of legal questions, not the least of which was the non-legal one of what attitude the courts would take toward it. Its framers were, therefore, unable to write the kind of law that either should have been written or that could be written today. It was not restrictive enough, for one thing—it allowed for a residential population of 77,000,000 in Greater New York and a working population even more astronomic.[2] It was clumsy in its method, in that it did not control density or bulk directly, required reference to three maps and much legal verbiage, and was not co-ordinated with either the State Tenement House Law or the City Building Code. But it held in the courts, and by 1927 John Nolen was able to report to the National Conference on City Planning,[3] of which he was President, that "The record shows that 176 cities, with a population of over 25,000,000 have been broadly replanned, for most of which accompanying plans have been printed. The greatest number of plans were prepared for cities of 50,000 to 100,000 population. Official zoning ordi-

---

[2] It is beginning to be conceded that these population figures are perhaps impossible of attainment. Revision of the zoning law has been proposed in 1944 by the New York City Planning Commission, which would reduce the possible population to 60,000,000 or thereabout. This drastic blow to real estate is being viewed with much alarm.

[3] "Twenty Years of City Planning Progress in the United States."

nances have been adopted by 525 cities. City planning commissions have been established in 390 cities."

More important than the statistics is the following: "The scope and character of city planning itself has changed in these twenty years. The local survey and the collection and interpretation of reliable data have become an essential part of good work. Facts and not guesses are the basis of recommendations. Plans and reports have been steadily improving. There is an advance in quality. The list of topics has been widened to include regional, state and even national planning." He reports "35 new towns, garden cities, suburbs or satellite towns," and the list includes Biltmore Forest, N. C., Coral Gables, Fla., Forest Hills, L. I., Kingsport, Tenn., Kohler, Wis., Longview, Wash., Mariemont, O., Roland Park, Md., Sunnyside, N. Y.—a widely dispersed list indeed, to which he could have added the notable "War Villages," among them one at Bridgeport, Ct., Yorkship Village near Camden, N. J., the developments at Newburgh, N. Y., Bath, Me., and elsewhere, the first ones in which American architects interested themselves in any other capacity than as monument builders or façade planners.

These were all, in greater or less degree, "planned communities," entities designed for living, and with a large measure of control over land use. In some cases only land was sold, and a few stores and other public structures were built by the developer; in some, houses and apartments were built or rented or sold. Control consisted of deed restrictions, ownership associations, or renting only instead of selling. Some were speculative, some were investments, some were glorified "company towns," but whatever their ultimate fate, they were planned as places in which to live a better life than was possible in the crowded heart of the city. It is a noteworthy fact that those which were so financed or otherwise organized as to retain the original land controls have survived as satisfactory places in which to live, while most of those which were not have succumbed in a large measure to blight through the intrusion of land uses not in conformity to their residential character or of residential building

of a type alien to the community.[4] As the writer has observed
elsewhere,[5]

> The "planned communities" of modern industry present
> a great range of size and purpose. Kingsport, Tenn. was
> planned as a strictly "business enterprise to build up the
> tonnage of the railroad and to yield profitable returns on
> the real-estate development," attracting as many and varied
> industries as possible. Nevertheless the development com-
> pany placed "particular emphasis . . . on the basic factor
> of planned economic development, guided by a real con-
> sideration of human interest, and with a view to ensuring
> a continuing and adequate supply of unspoiled and fairly
> treated labor." [National Resources Committee, op. cit.]
> It has become a large and completely independent city. The
> history of Longview, Washington, is similar.

At the other end of the scale are such completely company owned or dominated communities as Hopedale, Mass.,
or Chicopee, Ga., which are benevolent paternalities run
for the express purpose of maintaining satisfactory labor relations by supplying the worker with housing and an environment unobtainable elsewhere for the price.

What is notable is that all of these industrial projects
lay emphasis on the environment as well as the shelter.
Parks and playgrounds are provided, as well as schools, and
the company, even in the larger towns, such as Kingsport,
Longview, and Alcoa, has fostered and at times financially
assisted the establishment of hospitals, clubs, allotment
gardens and other community enterprises. In the smaller
developments these are often supplied entirely by the controlling company, with perhaps nominal charges for use.

These industrial towns and projects seem to definitely
demonstrate the value of unified and strong control of land-

---

[4] See National Resources Committee, *Urban Planning and Land Problems*,
for a thorough analysis of these developments.
[5] *Neighborhood Design and Control: An analysis of planned communities.*
Henry S. Churchill. National Committee on Housing, New York, 1944.

use. The appearance and integrity of the character of the development is rapidly lost in the towns which reverted to "normal" municipal practices, such as Kingsport, and Longview. Company-owned villages such as Hopedale, or even Alcoa (where most of the land is still company-owned although the government is normal), tend to retain the advantage of their plan.

It is also worth noting that these towns, except Kingsport and Longview which are full-fledged cities of over 20,000 population, are as stratified economically as the real-estate developments previously discussed or the government projects to be mentioned later. They could not, for the most part, exist as socially satisfactory communities were it not for the helping hand of their industries. The quality of the capital investment and the kind of social services that are present never could be supported by direct taxes on the householders.

The most notable of these planned communities was Radburn, N. J. Henry Wright and Clarence S. Stein were the town planners. It was a derivative of Howard's principles and Raymond Unwin's practices, but it contained entirely new elements. The chief of these were the complete segregation of automobile and foot traffic and the development of the superblock.[6] Here for the first time the automobile was considered as an essential fact to be coped with in a new way; here for the first time living was turned inward towards the rear and away from noise, here for the first time the safety of children was made of paramount importance. Through automobile traffic is kept away from the dwellings, which are grouped around a series of dead-end access roads. The houses face away from these roads, onto the interior of the large superblock, which provides means of interior foot-circulation to the school and shopping center through a series of parks. The main objection to this system is that neither side of the house has

[6] A "superblock" is a block of much greater than normal size, unpierced by through streets.

any privacy from passers-by, and more recent applications of the superblock idea have overcome this in various ways. The important point is that the super-block not only provides safety, but it also is more economical in the cost of streets and other utilities than the gridiron system, and permits a more rational use of land. Radburn was built at an unfortunate time, for the depression stopped its growth and nearly ruined its sponsors. The industry planned for it never came, and the development reverted to the status of a dormitory suburb instead of becoming the independent industrial town it was meant to be. But its planning principles have marched on.

Henry Wright was one of the great planners of his time. Besides his contribution to the war towns—a lovely little development outside of Newburgh, N. Y., is one of the best—he and Stein were the site planners for Sunnyside, Radburn, and the remarkable tour de force of Chatham Village outside of Pittsburgh. Sunnyside is an attempt to get some of the advantages of group planning within the framework of the city block by careful arrangement of the houses and the pooling of interior garden space. Chatham Village, also a white-collar row-house rental project, is on a difficult hillside site. The care and skill of the site planners and architects have produced a most charming place in which there is variety and graciousness as well as economy and simplicity. Wright also had potent influence on the Resettlement Administration's greenbelt towns. Wright never believed that "the good is better than the best," and his continual search for new approaches and methods of analysis often drove his colleagues to the verge of despair. For Wright had a fine and searching mind and he was extraordinarily sensitive to the subtle effects of the grouping of structures in relation to each other and to the rise and fall of land, of trees and water courses. Although not an architect, he did not see site planning and architecture as two different things, and he worked best in a team with sympathetic architects. His contributions to the techniques of low-cost housing and land planning were very consid-

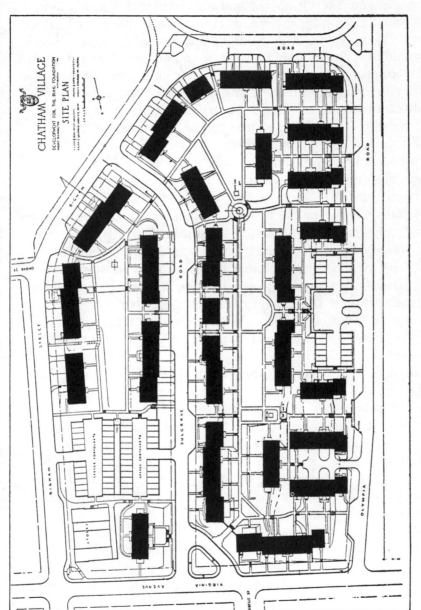

Plan of Chatham Village, Pittsburgh, Pa. Ingham and Boyd, architects; Henry Wright and Clarence S. Stein, site planners.

erable,[8] and it was his belief that no architect should be allowed to build a second housing project until he had lived at least six months in the first—a recommendation which, if followed, would probably result in the stuffing coming out of a lot of shirts. His comparatively early death was a serious loss to city planning, for although a most modest man and shy, he had a way of being stubborn as hell and Administrators listened to him with respect.

Satellite town building reached its culmination in Norris, Tenn., and the greenbelt towns. Strictly speaking, Norris was not a satellite town, but a community for the TVA personnel working on the Norris dam near Knoxville. It is now a dormitory town, as it has no industry of its own. Planned by Tracy Augur, it follows many of the Howard-Wright principles, modified to suit topographical and other conditions, and serves also as a workshop for many structural and organizational innovations.

The greenbelt towns built by the Suburban Resettlement Administration were in many ways among the most significant experiments of the early Roosevelt administration. There are three of them: Greenbelt, Md.; Greenhills, Ohio; Greendale, Wis., near Washington, Cincinnati, and Milwaukee. A fourth, Greenbrook, N. J., was designed, but its construction was stopped by injunction proceedings brought by the Liberty League at the behest of an irate local magnate who wanted "no wops and polacks" near his pre-revolutionary manor. They were a part of Rexford Guy Tugwell's vision of a future that is still distant, a vision doubly damned because it was Tugwell's and Roosevelt's.

Not that they presented any radicalism beyond that of Letchworth and Welwyn in England. They were to be planned communities, planned physically, economically, and politically; they were meant eventually to become completely independent on all three counts—self-contained, self-owned, and self-governed, free of all Federal control and taking their normal place in the county and state. They were perhaps the first towns in this country

---

[8] *Re-Planning Urban America* (Columbia University Press) is a basic technical reference book.

which were pre-planned by the co-operative endeavor of *all* the technics involved—from site selection to occupancy—through consultation between real-estaters, site planners, economists, architects, engineers, politicians, lawyers, management, construction men, and administrative and educational specialists. Even in the planning of Radburn technical advances had to yield in some measure to the conventional real-estate attitude, and the legal problems were much more difficult and restrictive because the houses were for sale.

The weak point of these greenbelt towns is the failure to provide for local industry and employment. Their sites were carefully chosen to be adjacent to industry, but the failure of industry to locate in Letchworth to the extent expected, the similar failure at Radburn and the disastrous attempts at rehabilitating "ghost towns" such as Arthurdale and others, led the administration to fight shy of repetition. Nevertheless, the lack of local industry is a definite handicap to the wholesome development of a community.

These towns, therefore, differed administratively from the normal town only in that the land was to be held by the town itself, and not by individuals. Any increment of value was to accrue to the town, and complete control of land-use was to be permanent. Thus it was sought to avoid the pitfalls of "co-operation." So far, the promise seems to be fulfilled.

Just before the war, a new Federally sponsored type of co-operative was projected, called "Mutual Home Ownership." The basic principle was again the acquisition of the property by co-operative societies (in this case labor unions), which would sell stock in the enterprise to the residents. Control rested in the trustees. Provisions were made for rebates for good maintenance, for carrying tenants over periods of unemployment or sickness, and for redemption or transfer of the stock in case of death or removal to other places. As families expanded or contracted they were to be moved to houses of suitable size. Rentals were established so as to provide for mutual protection against these contingencies, and were worked out on an actuarial basis subject to modification as experience accumulated. Besides this insurance feature, the rent of course covered the gradual acquisition of the property from the government, taxes and maintenance. Four of these groups have been established, and transfer from government to the societies is under way. This is a gradual process which follows the shifting interest between mortgagor (the government) and owner (the union) as the owner's equity increases through amortization. How successful these projects will be remains to be seen. Although the physical planning is good, there are many elements in the economic scheme that need further trial. Probably no such scheme can be fully successful on so small a base. As with any insurance, a wide spread of risk is necessary for financial safety, and from the tenant's point of view, flexibility of location—i.e., the ability to transfer from a "Mutual" in say Camden, to one in St. Louis or New Orleans—is almost as important. One thing is certain: without the financial backing of the Federal Government (or some other very large aggregation of capital, such as an Insurance Company), such a scheme would not even be possible.

The progress in the planning of new towns which resulted in Norris and the greenbelt towns had no counterpart in the planning, or rather re-planning, of existing cities. As Nolen noted, the technique of surveys and fact gathering improved, the relation of municipal economics to expansion, blight, traffic, and the rest were explored, but scarcely a single city carried out, except in minor details, any "plan" that was drawn up. Of the 135 published reports, nearly every one was filed in the City Engineer's office and forgotten. Chicago, Kansas City, St. Louis, and a few others were exceptions; but even these carried out only plans relating to large and spectacular public works: real re-planning, re-building of blighted residential areas, commercial slums, dreary wastes of semi-industrial stagnation, were not even attempted. The more typical fate of plans and commissions is related in George Dudley Seymour's "Letter of Resignation from the New Haven Commission on the City Plan." Written in 1924, after ten years as a member of the Commission,

Seymour resigned because, even though the terms of the Charter under which the Commission was established made planning "mandatory," the successive Mayors (who were Chairmen ex-officio) refused to let the Commission function. There were only thirty-five meetings in eleven years, and the original report on the City Plan, prepared by Cass Gilbert and Olmstead, was never acted upon in any way.

Daniel Burnham prepared a plan for San Francisco, which was completed a few years before the earthquake. As was the case with Wren's plan for London after the Great Fire, nothing was done about it, despite the until then unparalleled opportunity. There was no possible way to overcome the legal obstacles involved in re-apportioning land. Nor did Baltimore act after its fire. A survey made in 1923 under the direction of Henry V. Hubbard notes that the plans for San Francisco, Worcester, Bridgeport, Utica, and many others, were not followed in a single detail.

In most cases the economic motive for action was lacking. The economic waste of slums and blight was not a matter of which the public, nor even the municipal officials, were aware; indeed, except for obvious traffic-blocks which inconvenienced the public, there was little or no realization of the indirect costs of bad traffic conditions. Consequently the cities, after spending money on studies of highways and bridges, street car routes and parking needs, were under no pressure to do much about them. The grandiose Civic Centers languished from lack of funds and because reform in politics had taken the essential gravy out of them. The Pennsylvania boys had gone too far when they paid for lead-filled chandeliers by weight when cleaning up on the Capitol in Harrisburg. There was more and safer money in tearing up and repaving streets and building sewers. In a few cities the Civic Centers were started, either because of real necessity for consolidation of city departments or because a group of rich and public-spirited citizens provided funds for some of the necessary accessory buildings—such as a museum, library, or civic auditorium. Nevertheless, in the face of the great buzz-

buzz about planning, the net results have been startlingly meagre.

This brings up the nub of the question, what is wrong with city planning, why the good intentions and the complete lack of action? There seem to be several reasons besides the economic one noted above. Talbot Hamlin has brilliantly analyzed the public opinion angle in a paper, "A Public Opinion for Planning," published in the Summer of 1943 issue of the *Antioch Review*. He lists four major reasons:

> . . . the failure of the planners to enlist the active support of the great body of people for whom they have been planning.
>
> . . . the measuring of all values by the government debt and the tax rate . . . so that no popular backing is built up for improvements which might ultimately pay for themselves in cheaper transportation and lessened maintenance, not to speak of the vast improvements in living conditions they would buy.
>
> . . . a fear of planning as somehow undemocratic. This is based on a fundamental fallacy—that planning by the small boards of great corporations or of other financial pressure groups over which the citizen has no control is somehow "more American" than planning by governmental agencies over which he exerts more power than he realizes.
>
> . . . the notion that government planning for human values is destructive of private property, and especially of private initiative.

These are largely negative reasons, but in addition there are positive reasons: planning is a prerogative of those powerful vested interests "over which the citizen has no control" who use it quite naturally and very effectively for their own purposes. Such planning may range all the way from a small corporation making market surveys for future raw material purchases to the vast and complicated economic, physical, and population surveys, laboratories and services of such public utilities as A.T. and T. or the even more complicated and far-flung machinations of the oil and airways corporations. Such planning is taken for granted: similar planning by the government, particularly when it includes social considerations, is not to be tolerated. Government planning is assailed as regimentation, Communism, or Fascism. A minor eddy of this is the opposition of real estate groups to city planning and housing which, however, is lessened under the pressure of economic collapse. A drowning Economic Royalist thinks a life preserver looks pretty good, even if labeled "U.S. Coast Guard"—until safe ashore again and dry, when he begins to boast about how he got to land in spite of the lousy lead-filled government hand out.

Another reason why city planning has largely failed in accomplishment is that the planners themselves have been too preoccupied with statistics and the dry bones of their work. They have failed from lack of imagination. Their plans are soggy and lacking in fire, they have neither guts nor gusto. Planning consequently has failed to fire the public imagination and, failing that, has not been able to obtain the necessary legislation and administrative support, as Hamlin notes. There have been notable exceptions: the Lakefront development in Chicago, the East River Drive and Moses' Parkways in New York for example—spectacular affairs, like Haussmann's Boulevards, circuses and cake, but no bread, leaving the great living areas of the cities virtually unaffected. They are grand accomplishments but mean nothing in actual betterment to New York's Lower East Side or to Chicago's hundred square miles of slums and slime, or to the people of other hundreds of cities that are in need of bread and cannot afford circuses. What has been done in the way of amelioration of living conditions has been sporadic and planless, and has been done not as a part of a City Plan, but as part of a "slum clearance" program in which all collateral planning problems have been ignored, or if not ignored, pushed aside as irrelevant.

Perhaps, too, the professional planners have become bogged down in the survey and the statistic, so lauded by Nolen, so necessary as background and for a true understanding of what is needed, but never a substitute for vision. They have sought the comfort of the unassailable fact to be presented to the keen-eyed executive, and so have missed the excitement of inciting the voters to riot. Warren Vinton, the Federal Public Housing Authority's leading researcher, once defined Research as "the accumulation of irrelevant statistics in order to proceed from an unwarranted hypothesis to a foregone conclusion." It is also, often, merely an abracadabra for the obvious and a cloak for incompetence on a higher and more creative level.

City planning must go beyond statistics and street systems, housing and hooey. There is little to be gained by re-arranging discomfort, nor does it then matter much what form the re-arrangement takes. It hardly seems worth while to change things if they are to remain the same.

4. PROBLEMS

THE PROBLEMS WHICH NEED TO BE RESOLVED IN THE REMAKING
of our cities are complex, and particularly so in a democracy
where full play is given to the many counter currents of special
interests which are its life blood. There have been no examples
of city re-planning in the few democratically governed states of
the past, so that we today must guide ourselves not by the precedent of Nero, Sixtus V, and Haussmann, but by the method
of trial, error, and reconciliation.

Basically our difficulties are physical, due to too rapid growth
and to extraordinary industrial and scientific developments in
the last hundred and fifty years. A hundred and fifty years ago
—five short generations—the total population of the United
Kingdom was only 16,200,000, of London 959,000, of Paris,
553,000, of New York City, 60,000. In 1942 the count was,
United Kingdom, 47,889,000; Greater London, 8,200,000;
Greater Paris, 4,900,000; New York City (the five boroughs)
7,455,000. It is not to be wondered that the problems of physical
planning are immense and unsolved. Nor have economics, law
or the quasi-sciences of sociology and government kept abreast
of the times, and their failure to do so complicates and delays
physical action in city re-planning.

The specific problems which cities face vary, of course, from
city to city, but nevertheless there is a broad pattern common

to three categories of cities, which roughly may be classified as the small city, the big city and megalopolis. The lines of demarkation between these are shadowy, but as each is recognizable in general there is no need to try to specify "small," "big," and "biggest."

The small city generally has problems only of a more or less transient nature, i.e., economic difficulties dependent on the general "business cycle." Physically, most small cities are adequate, except perhaps for problems resulting from automobile traffic. Some have blighted areas or even small slums, and most of them suffer from over expansion of business areas—a form of lack of land use control which also accounts for mixed land uses detrimental to specific areas. In any event, the small city with healthy industry or commerce presents no problem that cannot be solved with reasonable determination, except in a few instances where special conditions prevail.

These are the small cities that have, for one reason or another, retrogressed or become stagnant. Savannah is an example of a seaport that long ago lost its position in world trade when the steamboat supplanted the sailing vessel, and never recovered its means of livelihood. Ironically enough, the first steam vessel to make the transatlantic voyage was the S.S. *Savannah*, from Savannah to Liverpool. Fall River, Mass., has lost its industry to cheaper labor markets, as has many another New England mill town; Troy, N. Y., and other Hudson River Valley cities have turned sour because regional shifts or technological changes have taken their industry elsewhere. There are many such places in the length and breadth of the States, not ghost towns—for they have no spirit—but towns just lost from the current of vigorous life. Although there is nothing essentially wrong with the fact that a city has ceased to grow, if it lacks the healthy vigor of industry and commerce stagnation results and, eventually, actual physical decay. In such cities there has been no replacement at all in the old central residential areas, or indeed in the business section. Their industrial plant is as obsolete and inadequate for modern use as their business buildings are for commerce and their old residence districts for living. The earlier expansion of industry and the intrusion of railroads has usually left a jumble of land uses which must be sorted out, re-planned and controlled, with new civic and social objectives in mind. These objectives will be hard for many small cities to swallow, based as they must be on recognition of the fact that population is static and that industry and commerce have stabilized at a constant level. The new objectives are, quite simply, the development of broadly humane and cultural satisfactions. To-day this does not mean provincialism—which, in many ways it would have meant even thirty years go—but an integration with the surrounding region rather than a greedy hope of dominating it. The energy that was formerly devoted to physical growth can now make for maturity.

The big city, on the other hand, shares the manifold problems of Megalopolis—all of them in some degree, although perhaps not to as great a degree. These problems are of three kinds: physical, economic, social, and each centers around three major factors: (1) habitation, working facilities, traffic; (2) land values, service costs, taxation; (3) child raising, health and recreation, social satisfactions.

1. Physical problems are, as has been said, an inheritance of unregulated, over optimistic and speculative growth. The older residential portions of the city suffer from overcrowding of the land and lack of organized open spaces for common or private use. In many instances this is not the result of too high densities of population so much as just plain bad use of land—too many streets, too many alleys, too much building coverage, not enough playground. The gridiron pattern contributes to this, with its lack of differentiation between traffic needs of various intensity and speed and its failure to provide satisfactory variation in sites and locations for different uses of land. In New York City, for instance, 35.55 per cent of the land is in streets, whereas 25 per cent would be fully sufficient. In Chicago, the great depth of the standard block forced deep, narrow building lots and back alleys. At the same time, vast areas of the business portion

of most cities are empty—devoted to parking lots, or to a solitary "dining car," or to junk yards. Stores are empty, loft buildings are deserted.

The actual working facilities are also important. The industrial plants of many cities are obsolete, so are a great part of the business and commercial structures. Consider any "Main Street," the stores have had their faces lifted by "modern" fronts, but the second, third (and often more) stories above are run down and dingy. There is, everywhere, too much business area. One can name principal streets in almost any city, Camden's Broadway, Cleveland's Euclid, Buffalo's Delaware, Main Street anywhere, vast sections of New York, Philadelphia, Boston.

The skyscraper fad also did much harm to the business centers of cities. Aside from the extreme examples, few of which have paid their way (according to the Urban Land Institute there are about five hundred buildings over twenty stories in height in the United States, none of which has been successful financially [1]), the crop of lesser skyscrapers has brought financial disaster to the surrounding properties. Two quotations, one from an Urban Land Institute study of Louisville, Ky.,[2] the other from a similar study of Milwaukee, Wis.,[3] will point this up.

There is a unanimity of informed opinion in Louisville that the development of skyscrapers during the 1920's was one of the principal reasons for the decline of values in the central business district. This type of development created a very unbalanced distribution of land use, which was detrimental to the rest of the downtown property. It would be far better if, when additional business facilities are needed, they are provided by a horizontal, rather than a vertical, expansion. This can be brought about by the revision of zoning regulations and it is strongly recommended here.

Reduce height regulations in the central business district

[1] *Urban Land Institute Bulletin* for February, 1943.
[2] Urban Land Institute *Proposals for Downtown Louisville.*
[3] Urban Land Institute *Proposals for Downtown Milwaukee.*

to an absolute maximum of between 85 and 100 feet, the exact figures to be determined by a careful study of actual needs by the Board of Public Land Commissioners. In applying this regulation, the underlying motive should be to spread out the substantial land use of the central area, so that it will ultimately restore the full usefulness of the numerous lots now vacant or simply used for parking purposes.

Integration of work and living rarely exists. In general, the present zoning laws, designed to "protect" high-class residential neighborhoods, prevent any adequate attempts at solving the problem. Such zoning is designed to keep land uses in separate categories by progressive exclusion—that is, starting from an undifferentiated area permitting any use, various classes of industry, business, etc., are excluded until the Simon pure single family house district is reached. Under this system of classification, which usually calls for rigid and inflexible mapping, it is very difficult to plan integrated neighborhoods or communities. Another difficulty, to be dealt with more fully later, is that no way has as yet been devised for dealing with the non-conforming use, once it has been permitted to intrude; nor does it keep residences out of industrial or factory use areas. The latter mixture has resulted in some of the worst of city slums and unhealthy conditions. Zoning must be devised to encourage integrated relationships of land uses, which is a very different thing from the indiscriminate scrambling of them, which is encouraged under the present system except in the exclusively residential areas.

The rapid transformation of zoning from an instrument of public welfare to a protective device for vested interest is attested by a report written in 1924, eight years after the enactment of the New York City Building Zone Resolution. This report, written under the chairmanship of Clarence S. Stein, was made to the Fifty-seventh Annual Convention of the American Institute of Architects. Part of it is worth quoting here, as an intervening period of twenty years has merely intensified the points made in it:

The initial move in the case of zoning American cities was justified on the ground that industry and business, in the course of growth and expansion, blighted residential areas or passed over and completely destroyed them. Zoning would prevent all this. The necessity for conserving residential areas was a matter of the common welfare and so it was conceived that zoning could be put into effect and enforced by the exercise of police power. What constitutes police power is, of course, rather vague, but it was conceived that zoning fell within it.

The theory of zoning was thus a very simple one. In making an application of the theory, however, the practice of zoning immediately passed beyond the matter of conserving that which would accrue to the advantage of the common welfare and proceeded to utilize the principle and the power to conserve, stabilize and enhance property values. And it is upon the efficacy of zoning as a measure which will stabilize or enhance property values that its popularity has come to hang. Has any proposed zoning ordinance the slightest possibility of going into effect unless it is so framed that it is obvious that pecuniary gains will follow to the owners of property through its enactment?

Now, pecuniary gains seldom arise out of withdrawing land from the possibility of industrial or business use. So resort is had to the creation of many residential categories so as to provide finely graded areas of differential exclusiveness. In this way, property values are stabilized and enhanced. This consideration now furnishes the main ground for the popularity of zoning.

If we turn back to the original concept it is clear that zoning as it is now carried on can hardly be justified on the ground that, by and large, it serves the interest of the common welfare. It may be that the segregation of economic classes is quite the reverse. In any event, whether the practice as developed is for good or evil, it is perfectly evident that the constitutional ground upon which zoning was originally based has been cut away by the creation of an ever increasing number of categories. . . .

On the other hand, from the standpoint of the architect, zoning has imposed innumerable restrictions, many of them futile and unimportant which tend to increase the complexity of his task in planning for the use of property, often preventing the introduction of desirable innovations suggested by an intelligent appreciation of his problem. So rigid are these rules in many of our prominent zoned cities and so little have they to do with the essential principles of community planning that a well conceived Town Planning and Housing Scheme, on the lines of the best Dutch and English precedents, would be possible only in new districts which have not yet been trimmed up by the procrustean ax of the zoning expert.

In sum, the only rational end for which zoning can exist, namely, to promote better communities for living and working and bringing up children, is actually often hindered by the present applications of zoning. Need we wonder that current city planning has so little interest for the architect?

The character of the factory is changing (except for certain of the primary "heavy" industries) and the method of planning residential areas is also changing. A new type of zoning must be evolved, which will permit, or rather insist, that the two get together, or the transportation problem will remain unsolvable. An attempt to work this out in New York City has met with the most violent and reactionary opposition. The City Planning Commission approved a zoning change to permit an electrical research laboratory, with a small housing development for the workers, in a residential district. The plan was carefully worked out for low density and to protect the public interest by guaranteeing public access to the "campus." Yet short-sighted property owners fought it tooth and nail. Such developments, with proper safeguards, should increase the demand for neighboring residential property, not decrease or depreciate it.

Further, in considering this matter of living and working, very little thought has been given to the fact that in the large cities over half of the population works in what is called "service industry," business and government, that is, they are "white collar workers" and highly skilled labor. The residential location in relation to the place of employment of the workers in a department store or large insurance company employing six to eight hundred people is as important as that of the same number of workers in a factory. No effort has as yet been made to handle this problem, possibly because "white collar workers" are considered super-proletarian by themselves, and sub-human by their employers.

Lack of integration is responsible for a good part of the traffic difficulties which beset city and nation—difficulties in the movement of people and of goods. This problem has been the one most vigorously attacked everywhere, but the attack has been without much effect because the basic plan has been untouched. The traffic planner who takes traffic counts and then recommends a series of street widenings and lights and intersection remodelings is like a doctor who takes bloodcounts and then recommends an old-fashioned bleeding as a remedy for arteriosclerosis. Solution must be by way of complete diagnosis: railroads, markets, docks, airports, congested areas, and recreational areas must be brought into some kind of proper relation with each other, the lines of future growth plotted, and controls put into effect. The design of streets and highways does not make sense unless the land use along them, and at their terminations, is strictly regulated to suit the type and kind of traffic for which they are designed.

The coming of the cheap car, the subsidizing of the automobile business through the building of vast networks of paved roads—first macadam, then concrete, first two lanes, then three, then four or more—made the accommodation of this traffic a naturally primary concern of cities and towns. Streets were widened, by-passes provided, municipal parking lots established. All to no avail, because the problem was only partially thought through. The new arteries immediately became choked, because the secondary routes were deemed unsatisfactory or difficult by the traveling public, and because the easier it was made to get some place else, the more people wanted to go. "Sunday driving" as a phenomenon can be explained rationally only one way —the places people live in are so unpleasant almost any discomfort of hot and crowded roads seems better, their recreational opportunities and inner resources are so slight and so poor that movement of any kind any place is at least one degree more tolerable than "staying put."

Trucking also brought new problems. In the cities loading and unloading created congestion in industrial areas, just as parking clogged circulation in business districts. In the small towns the trucks created a monstrous hazard, particularly in "one street" towns and villages which had grown naturally along a highway. The towns could, and did, institute some measure of police control, but the villages became mere points on a high-speedway. In both cases, once pleasant and often beautiful residential sections were ruined. Tourist cabins, tourist homes, "motels," filling stations, cheap eating places and roadside stands took the place of the once decent homes and of the old trees that were ruthlessly cut down to provide an additional traffic lane.

Failure to consider anything except traffic relief has produced some unfortunate results in the past—unfortunate in the long run for the city, although satisfactory enough for the speculator in outlying land. The immediate effect of the extension of rapid transit facilities, whether in the form of trolley car, subway, or express highway, is to open up cheap land for speculative development. It was formerly thought that such development was what paid for the facility, by adding to the city tax-roll. During the period of expansion there was a great deal to this theory: with a stabilizing population it falls apart completely, since the principal source of peripheral population is from the center of the city. The most obvious example is probably Queens Borough, which has grown enormously, thanks to the Independent Subway and Commissioner Moses' highways—largely at the expense of Manhattan, which has not grown appreciably.

The airplane is bringing new problems. Where should airfields be located in relation to residential areas, industry and other shipping facilities such as railroad freight yards? As yet there are no clear answers indicated, because the airplane is in the process of development, and we do not know what the future will bring. All that can be done is to provide facilities for the immediate present, knowing full-well that mistakes will be made of the same kind that were made in the early days of the railroads. The plane of today bears the same relation to the plane of tomorrow that the locomotive of the '50s bore to the electric or diesel giant of today. The early railroads brought problems of noise, smoke, and danger at crossings which have only been eliminated as technical developments have been made and capital invested. The airplane of today is insufferably noisy and the landing fields required are too big in proportion to the commerce. Nevertheless, the situation must be met as it exists, even if it proves to be all wrong in twenty years. Physical planning cannot anticipate unprecedented developments in other technics.

2. Economic problems are obviously related to the physical, and on into the social. The legacy of speculative "values" has most cities tied up in knots. The collapse in urban land values is due to two things. The rate of growth of cities has slowed up. The automobile has increased, in geometrical ratio to its commuting radius, the amount of accessible land. Assessments which were made on the basis of hoped-for growth and desired scarcity are no longer related to any real fact. Slums and blighted areas, the ones most in need of rehabilitation, or rather re-planning, are just the ones where these left-over values are highest. It is a paradox of our tax system that the earning capacity of urban land is not necessarily reflected in its assessment. Theoretically, the assessment reflects earning capacity in the sense that there is obviously more earning capacity in a good central location than in a distant one and assessment practices do take into account, to some extent, the age and character of the building. Actually, the assessed

values of the land are so tied up with the constitutional bonded indebtedness of cities, and their limited ability to raise taxes, that any material reduction in assessments, no matter how justified in fact, would mean municipal bankruptcy.

The effect of this paradox on residential areas is well understood. It is a cause as well as an effect of blight, and like a malignant disease spreads its poison. It is in large part responsible for the fact that public housing has not only failed to clear slums to any great extent, but rather has encouraged blight by forcing local housing authorities either to purchase outlying land or resort to the use of extremely high population densities on central sites. No public housing project has ever reduced the density on the site; in New York City densities have been doubled or trebled. The same over-building is true of course of private enterprise housing, but we are so used to taking that for granted that it elicits no comment; public housing, however, is supposed to serve public purposes in the broad sense as well as the particular one of providing shelter. This it cannot do as long as a fictitious value dictates the intensity of use, instead of the optimum intensity of use establishing the value. Every city, regardless of size, has the paradox of property which has been rotting, literally, for years, being so highly "valued" by the municipality and consequently by the courts in condemnation proceedings, that development is impossible at densities suitable to the over-all pattern of the city and therefore to its best interests.

It is often argued that the amount of public housing is so small that it makes no difference to the city pattern; but private enterprise is caught on the horns of the same dilemma. It resorts to developing cheap, outlying land. This may be either within the city limits, along newly constructed transportation lines, as in Queens; or in completely suburban subdivisions, as has been the case in every big city and many smaller ones. It is the only way middle income families, who constitute the largest market for private enterprise, can be supplied at all. In boom times past this sub-divisioning went on at a terrific rate. Thousands upon thousands—literally—of lots were platted and supplied with the minimum of utilities. They were sold on all sorts of bases—outright, time, mortgage, with an extra lot thrown in for the first purchasers, and so on. Hundreds of thousands of these lots remain unsold or unbuilt on, the marked out streets choked with weeds.[4] Chicago alone had some twelve square miles of vacant subdivided area, much of it improved with streets and utilities; in New Jersey there were 185,000 platted acres, enough for over a million fifty by one hundred foot lots; the State of California held tax deeds for 64,200 subdivided lots.

Still other subdivisions were half successful, just sufficiently so for the city to be forced into providing police, fire protection, schools, garbage collection, and other services. Tax returns, in such cases, did not anywheres near meet the cost, yet the services had to be provided.

"Speculative subdivisions, wherein the developer is primarily interested in selling lots as cheaply as possible, eventually create conditions, the remedies for which are very expensive to the public authorities. Such subdivisions in competition with sound, well-improved developments result in great damage to land values throughout the entire City. The cost of providing public service to badly located and poorly designed, premature subdivisions will eventually cause excessively high taxes throughout the community and will add great complications to the orderly development of a well-balanced City."[5]

When private enterprise does build on central city land, it does so only when two principal conditions can be met. There must be a market for relatively high-rental apartments, and the lot must be built up to the legal capacity. The latter point also has two aspects. For extremely high rents the number of people housed is not too great, perhaps, but the bulk of the building is kept at the maximum because of the size of the rooms. The

[4] See Philip H. Cornick, *Problems Created by Premature Subdivisions of Lands in Selected Metropolitan Areas.* Division of State Planning, Albany, N.Y., 1938. Also, *Premature Land Subdivision, A Luxury.* New Jersey State Board of Planning. 1941.

[5] *Proposals for Downtown Louisville*; a study published by the Urban Land Institute.

building bulk for lower rentals remains the same, and the population increases because the same total rental return must be squeezed out by making the apartments themselves as small as will be tolerated. In both cases light, air and open space are reduced to the minimum, and in the second case the increase in population overcrowds common public facilities of every sort.

In the case of blighted commercial and industrial sections, the story is a little different. Lack of land control, too loose zoning where zoning starts, have permitted altogether too much commercial space in our cities, and in many of them the industrial structures are largely obsolete. In some cities business frontage runs as high as fifty front feet per hundred persons. This is outside of the central downtown shopping center which also serves the surrounding region and so is able to sustain more business. Various studies have pointed out that even the more usual amount of twenty-five front feet per hundred is too much for purely local business, that there is an excess of vacancies and of marginal businesses that do not hold their own for long and produce an enormous turn-over of tenants. Ten to fifteen front feet per hundred persons, in the opinion of many, would be ample for the needs of the average community, including an ample amount for those venturesome souls who like to invest their capital in certain failure. Manufacturing and loft space is also suffering, not as much from over-production as from inadequacy. Buildings are badly lighted, poorly elevatored, too full of columns to permit installation of modern machinery, or with too heavy wall construction to permit flexibility and too light a floor system to support heavy machinery. Traffic congestion, inadequate shipping facilities, insufficient parking space have blighted entire areas. Then, too, business has had a tendency to concentration into larger units, best exemplified by the chain stores, while industry is continually improving its techniques, and requires less space to produce more goods. Many kinds of factories are requiring a different kind of space, more spread out to facilitate assembly and with plenty of open land for parking. Methods of merchandising have changed, and warehousing is no longer as

important as it once was since the motor truck has provided release from the railroad siding. On the other hand, the motor
truck itself requires facilities for loading and unloading, which
are hard to meet in the old parts of cities without using the
streets for loading and thereby clogging traffic.

Wholesale abandonment of space, of course, reflects back into
the tax rate, and reflects back regardless of whatever the taxes
may be, ad valorem real estate levies or something else. The objection to the ad valorem tax is that it freezes a false base of so-
called "values," and consequently prevents any attempts at
readjustment to a rational use based on income. Moreover, a
maximum tax rate is usually written into the state law, and often
a debt limit is also set, which bears a direct relation to the total
assessed value of real estate. In boom times owners want high
assessments and low rates for the obvious reason that then the
assessment bolsters the high asking price and the low tax rate
appears to be an inducement. When times get bad and the market is dull, then the high assessments become a burden and serve
to slow the market still more—yet that is when the city must
raise its tax rate if it is to keep going, and the high assessment
proves a boomerang.

What is usually overlooked is the simple, essential fact that
city services must somehow be paid for, and that "the tax rate is
not, in itself, important. Dollars are what really matter. When
the tax levy remains the same, the tax rate will go up when assessed valuation goes down; and the tax rate will go down when
assessed valuations go up." [6] But, when the bonded indebtedness
is tied to the valuation, the assessments cannot go down materially without bringing technical bankruptcy regardless of the
municipal income, and if the assessments remain up property
cannot change hands and rehabilitation cannot take place, and
consequently taxes cannot be collected except from "strong"
foreclosure holders such as banks. The circle is as deadly as
nightshade.

[6] Town of Montclair, N.J.: A Study in Municipal Service and Finance. The
Princeton Surveys, Princeton University, 1942.

A good many schemes have been brought forward to try and break this circle. All the so-called "Urban Redevelopment" plans for financial aid to cities are aimed at this: how to bridge the gap between an acquisition cost which will keep values up for the owners, assessments up for the cities, and a use-value that will permit a legitimate profit to the builder and operator. The answers have all been along the same line: 1) Municipalities must be empowered to purchase land and re-sell it or lease it for long periods; 2) they must be financially aided in acquiring the land by the Federal Government; 3) such land must be re-developed by private enterprise, under varying degrees of control by the municipality or its agency. By some device, usually long-term federal credit, the difference between cost at assessed valuation and use-value, is absorbed. There are many who think the differential should be written off by federal grant. In other words, society must pay today and tomorrow for the errors of society yesterday; the land-owner today must not suffer, nor the mortgagee, nor anyone. Mr. Alvin Hansen once stated it quite succinctly:[7]

> We argue that the passage of laws radical enough to squeeze out quickly the whole of these excesses of valuation would be politically impossible, and of doubtful desirability even if possible. Society as a whole, we submit, is mainly responsible for the conditions existing, and society as a whole should pay the cost of cleaning them up so a fresh start can be made. The problem is not unlike that confronting Alexander Hamilton when he proposed the assumption by the federal government of the states' Revolutionary debts.

This might be fair enough if the fresh start proposed were to offer a new outlook. Unfortunately, most of the proposals are such that they would result, in thirty or fifty years, in exactly the same intolerable mess as that in which we now find ourselves.

Moreover, all plans, so far, for urban redevelopment, leave untouched the other half of the fiscal quandary—the *ad valorem*

[7] From an article in the *National Municipal Review*, February, 1943.

base of real estate as the principal revenue source. It is not that this quandary is unappreciated; there is endless argument about it and a large and growing sentiment in favor of a shift to what are coming to be called "occupancy tax principles." The trouble is that the framers of urban redevelopment legislation cannot incorporate the necessary tax system changes in their bills, because almost everywhere such changes would require amendments to the state constitution. Yet, without tax reform, urban redevelopment must fail of its main purpose, which is urban redevelopment and not just the bailing out of property owners.

There are many corollary aspects of the cost of municipal services and the tax rate—the use of city facilities by non-residents, for instance, of which the use of municipal parking lots by "foreign" cars is an example; the carrying of useless civil service employees on the city payroll because of mandatory legislation or tender court decisions; other kinds of expenses made mandatory by state legislatures; failure of state government to return a just share of collected taxes, and many others—such as duplication and over-lapping of governmental functions. A metropolitan region may have several hundred governmental and administrative units, many of which not only overlap in function, but overlap in their physical boundaries, so that confusion is twice confounded, and because of inertia or jealousy little in the way of planning can even be planned. Every city has its own special kind of problems in this field, and every tax expert has his own special solutions. Some sort of solution must indeed be found, for physical replanning by itself is a snare and a delusion; physical replanning must be part and parcel of the economic framework, or it is meaningless, or it has an ill meaning, like pouring water down a rat hole.

The whole question of the costs of civic service needs further exploration and a breathing in of fresh air untainted by the bemused recalcitrance of politicians. The relation between per capita income and cost of services must be clarified. The cost of schooling, for example, is alone in excess of what the average family can afford to pay in taxes. The majority of the population (except in the cases of a very few wealthy areas, such as West-chester County for example), cannot afford the actual cost of schools plus other services plus cost of maintaining their homes. In Boston, for instance, the cost of schooling runs as high as $127 per pupil; in New York City, for the high schools, it is $159 per pupil. The great majority of taxpayers cannot afford to pay anything like this for education, to say nothing of the cost of all the other municipal services. Taxes on a $5000 dwelling unit —whether a single family house or urban apartment makes no difference—cannot very well exceed (and seldom equal) $150 per year. Not over 15% of families in the United States can afford even a $5000 dwelling: 85% of the families have incomes of *less* than the $2500 a year which, according to usually accepted rules of thumb is tops for ownership of a $5000 home, or an annual rental of $625. For the still lower income families, the burden of rent or ownership can only be met at the rule of thumb level by excessive sacrifices of food, clothing and general health. The majority of families are therefore unable to meet the tax bill, and they are very largely subsidized by the wealthy, the industries, and the resources of the state. New York State, for example, contributes an average 22.4% to the cost of local government throughout the state: it varies from 18.4% contributed to New York City to 44.1% contributed to 26 of the poorer counties.[8] Where such aid is not provided, education and city services sink to the level of those southern states where there is neither wealth nor industry upon which to draw for subsidy.

The relation of this problem of land value, peripheral drift, and ability to pay, to the physical municipal plant has been analyzed in a pioneering and extremely acute study by F. Dodd McHugh, Director of Planning of the New York City Planning Commission, "Cost of Public Services in Residential Areas." His study shows an astonishingly high degree of obsolescence in the physical plant necessary for city services—schools, sewers, utilities of all kinds, together with a lack of parks and open areas other

[8] The source of most of this revenue is New York City, so that in effect that city is subsidizing the poorer communities of the state as well as its own poor.

than streets. Yet the cost to the city for reasonable rehabilitation is shown to be less than the construction of a precisely similar type new development on the periphery. Peripheral expansion thus compounds costs: the new area must be fully serviced, the old one cannot be abandoned. The new one will take years to reach an optimum population; the blighted old one is also insufficiently inhabited. It is worth quoting at length from the discussion which followed the reading of Mr. McHugh's paper before the American Society of Civil Engineers.[9] Mr. McHugh said:

Mr. Baker has noted the economic losses of individuals, property owners, and the public at large due to urban blight and decentralization. Incidentally, one phase of the original cost study indicated that over-expansion and duplication of public services in residential areas are costing the City of New York at least $40,000,000. annually for operation and maintenance. This is a rough estimate, to be sure, but it suggests the extent of economic loss suffered by the public as a result of blight and decentralization within the city's boundaries. Mr. Baker also mentioned the problem of land assembly and high site cost in connection with large-scale rebuilding. He asks if rents in a rebuilt area can support the high site cost and suggests that it might be a sound investment to subsidize such residential projects at least to the extent of overcoming the burden of high land acquisition costs. Here is one of the greatest obstacles to city rebuilding. It would appear questionable that even one community could be rebuilt privately on a large scale and become self-supporting without public financial assistance because the rentals that its tenants could afford are almost certain to be insufficient to cover the high site cost plus the expense of new dwelling construction. The ease of land assemblage and its relatively low cost in suburban and outlying urban areas permit profitable private developments, and account in

[9] American Society of Civil Engineers, Transactions, Vol. 107, 1942.

some measure for the continued physical expansion of cities even after population growth is drastically reduced.

He goes on with the following cogent analysis:

In rebuilding such obsolete sections on a large scale, it will be necessary to make provision for families of varying income. Assume that in the present case the engineer is concerned with an average community that will accommodate all groups. With this assumption it is possible to deal with the average rental that people can afford to pay. In New York City this sum is approximately $520. annually per family, which represents the average "demand." What can the private developer supply to meet this demand?

The answer to this question is conditioned in large measure by the capital outlay required of the private developer and the annual carrying charges on the completed project. For purposes of discussion, assume that the operation and maintenance, including insurance and a vacancy allowance, can be held to an average of $150. per dwelling unit. On the basis of the $520. average annual income received for each dwelling unit, and an annual cost of $150. for operation, etc., the private developer would have $370. left to cover taxes, capital charges, and interest on his equity.

Since the problem concerns a large-scale development that offers unusual stability of investment, it is possible that the private developer can obtain capital at 4% and, because the investor will want his capital repaid, the loan might be amortized at, say, 1.5% annually. With annual interest payments fixed at 4% and amortization at 1.5%, the borrower would repay the entire loan in about thirty-four years. This set-up is similar to recent financing under the FHA mortgage insurance plan.

The private developer also must receive a return on his equity of investment. In these days of low capital earning, one may assume a 6% return to be quite attractive. Inasmuch as the rebuilt community is a large-scale affair, requiring adequate public facilities on modern standards, the city could not afford to supply improvements and services without making some charge for them. Therefore, real estate taxes should be included in considering private costs. These private costs may be expressed as:

Item:	Percentage of total capital cost:
Interest	4 % on 80% or 3.2 %
Amortization	1.5 % on 80% or 1.2 %
Equity Earning	6.0 % on 20% or 1.2 %
Taxes	2.75% on 92% or 2.53%
Total	8.13%

The private developer received on the average only $370. per dwelling unit to cover these charges. This amount capitalized at 8.13% is $4,550. which represents the total private investment per dwelling unit that can be made economically in this particular case. In a large scale operation it may be possible to effect such economies that existing structures on the site could be demolished and the new dwellings erected at an average cost of $3,640. per family unit. For this "average" case this development cost is roughly 40¢ per cu. ft. At such a favorable rate for construction costs the private developer could afford to pay $910. per dwelling unit for land. If the community is built to house 250 persons per residential acre, land could not cost more than $1.42 per sq. ft.; at a density of 430 persons per residential acre, the developer could pay $2.45 per sq. ft. for land. At a density of 540 the economic value of land is slightly more than $3. per sq. ft. under these assumptions.

No further comment is necessary! And although the exact figures used by Mr. McHugh apply only to New York City, the same thing in ratio applies to every large city in the country. It should be noted also, that any element of extravagance or corruption in the city government can be largely discounted. Corruption affects capital expenditures primarily; and although the elimination of extravagance can somewhat reduce municipal operating costs in both new and old areas, the essential impossibility of the rehabilitation of central areas, in the face of land "values" which are quite unrelated to ability to pay, remains.

3. In the broad sense, neither physical nor economic planning has any meaning except in reference to social objectives. These objectives are, or should be, a city in which children can be raised and educated to become healthy, decent human beings; in which it is possible to earn a "living wage" with reasonable prospects of security; in which the amenities of life, social intercourse, amusement, recreation, and cultural advantages are procurable. It is not an Utopian ideal, by any means—many towns in the past and some in the present have approached it. The fact is, most people do not want a great deal of anything, nor have they fancy standards. A clean house, with room for family life, and privacy, a bit of ground for the children or adequate community playgrounds; a good school; a steady job that will feed, house, clothe, and doctor the family; the neighborhood movie, bowling alley, saloon; and the libraries, museums, theaters, or what not somewhere in the center of things. That is for the every-day living of the backbone of the city; the bright lights, the crowds, the tension of the market place, the intensity of metropolitan life with its luxury and vice are only the big show of the big centers, not their reality. They may be what attract people to the metropolis; they are what makes the little man puff out his chest and call his cousin from Littleburg a hick; they are what brings in the tourists and wastrels, but they are not what keeps a city going, and certainly not the towns.

The opportunity to exchange work, merchandise and ideas, these are primary to the concept of a city. It is the scale on which these things are humanly possible that has been lost sight of, and which must be restored.

Nor, in considering the social aspects, problems and objectives of the city should its esthetic qualities be forgotten. It is fashionable to sneer at the City Beautiful, it is fashionable to talk about city planning in terms of the cold, hard facts of economic impossibilities, in terms of pseudo-scientific approaches to density or to cost of services, or in terms of fatuous assumptions derived from highly dubious surveys. The planner or architect who whispers about doing something merely because it would be beautiful and delightful simply sticks his neck right under the knife. This attitude is part of that spiritual and moral degeneration of the moment which E. H. Carr [10] has so well described, and which Saarinen has discussed in detail from the architectural angle in his recent book.[11]

There is no use evading the question. Our cities, any and all, are at best glorifications of the ungracious. The gridiron plan will permit of nothing else, and the "civic centers" are mere agglomerations of diverse buildings. Separately beautiful buildings, unrelated spacially, do not make a beautiful city nor a beautiful civic center. One need only look at Foley Square in New York to see the truth of this dictum—it is the most revolting ugly public "square" in the world, and probably the most expensive. Copley Square in Boston is another example, though of a different order. There the contrast and interest in McKim's Library and Richardson's Trinity Church are damaged by the dull fronts of the Huntington Avenue stores and houses and by the incongruous mass of the Copley Plaza Hotel. Washington, which had opportunities, has been botched by the incompetence of the architectural profession in civic art. Philadelphia, New York since 1811, Cleveland, Denver, Los Angeles, Chicago, Fort Wayne, all those designed for speculation in land, never had a chance.

The anonymous critic, previously quoted on Washington, D.C., writing in the *American Journal of Science and Arts* in 1830, is worth again quoting at some length, for the acuteness of his criticism and the soundness of his observations:

> Beauty is not in favor of the rectangle. We should judge of the beauty of our city, more from its impression on strangers, than on ourselves. We are accustomed to its forms; its associations affect us; we are warped by our attachment to family and friends, and are no longer fit judges on the sub-

[10] E. H. Carr, *Conditions of Peace.*
[11] *The City: Its Growth, Its Decay, Its Future,* by Eliel Saarinen. Reinhold, 1943.

ject. We feel all this, and inquire with some anxiety of the stranger what he thinks of it. This may not always be perfectly polite, but the question is still natural enough, and we must only take care that intimacy or friendly confidence between us may warrant it. Who so capable of setting us right where we are wrong, as he who sees with other eyes, and hears with other ears, and who may properly be expected to judge with greater candor than ourselves? I say then we should watch the impression of our city on visitors, and learn wisdom from their remarks. A rectangular city, as far as its plan is concerned, will not be found to interest a visitor long. He understands it easily and its dimensions shrink: he turns angle after angle and it is all the same, till the houses take also this character of uniformity, and however beautiful, cease to interest. He looks along a street: it stretches far before him, and he feels as we do in looking up a long straight road—it may be very convenient but we feel no disposition to pursue it further, though it may be planted with elms and dressed with rich vines, and enlivened with the sweet melody of birds: we are just as well off where we are, why go further? But give that road a turn near us, and our curiosity is immediately excited to pursue it further. I recollect a road not far from Wooster in Ohio. It ran, I think, six or seven miles as straight as an arrow, and when I travelled on it, became at last absolutely painful to me. I began to feel like a man in a straight jacket, and perhaps the road contractors would have said I deserved one. But to return to our rectangular city. Every one will recollect his sensations, on turning from street to street, and finding the same long vistas before him. It may please for a few moments at first, but the feelings soon grow dull and stagnate, and he turns listlessly away. Such a city has two important principles of beauty, symmetry and neatness; but, in a city at least, variety is essential to beauty: this is uniform, and therefore soon becomes dull. We have variety, and nature has provided largely for it: no two scenes are alike, though

rocks, hills, trees, valleys and streams may go to the composition of both. We should soon tire of nature if things were
so, at least if they were often so. At a first visit to a spot, it
is the constant succession of new views taking us by surprise
and sharpening curiosity, that delights us: afterwards it is
this adaptation of forms to our nature, this variety suited
to our love of variety, that fixes itself so strongly on our
souls. Other principles of our nature, no doubt, are acted
on, but this is among the uppermost. Let us bring it to the
test. Suppose close together two beautiful scenes exactly
alike in all parts: they would excite our wonder, but apart
from this, would there not be a strong disappointment in
our feelings? Would not the one we saw first, sink in our
estimation because the other was just like it? Let us go
further: suppose there were three such, we should wonder
more for a short while and then begin to be indifferent:
four, we should begin to tire; five, we should be weary; six,
it would require an effort to look at them, and we should
then begin to dislike. I will change the case. Let the reader
suppose himself in a forest with a handsome glade by his
side: he turns and has one exactly like it by him again: a
few feet more and another comes; and again another, and
so on without end. Those trees might be different in shape
and in their leaves; but if disposed, as was said, exactly alike
in all cases, would he seek that forest again for a pleasant
walk? Again, suppose this variety of trees were disposed in
the form of uniform avenues, stretching far as the eye could
reach, would he then be greatly pleased? But suppose these
avenues in every variety, now broad and open, now shaded
and narrow, one while opening to a wide stretch of land-
scape, and at another pointing to a rocky glen: how our feelings change at the thought? This is the effect of variety. No
city then should be uniform, not even uniform in beauty, or
it will pall and tire. I love, myself, in traversing a city, to be
taken by surprise; to be able to anticipate some new form,
or combination of forms, at every turn; to have my admira-

tion constantly drawn upon by the taste and judgment shown in these combinations, and to have the city swell out and magnify its dimensions from my only half successful effort to comprehend them. A word or two on this last subject: it is of no great consequence, but should not be altogether neglected, in our discussion. Every one will recollect his surprise on ascending a steeple in an irregular town, or an adjoining eminence, and looking down on it to find it so small: it is but a short time since I took such a view of Hartford, and found it but little more than half as large as I had imagined. This is natural: the constant effect of partial obscuring is to magnify, and no one will neglect it when he wishes to strike us by the vast or grand.

That the difference between the beautiful and the ugly, the delightful and the squalid, the varied and the monotonous, has important psychological effects is a commonplace, except in the field of city planning. If it be not quoting the Devil for Scripture, Nietzsche has written: "All that is ugly weakens and afflicts man. It reminds him of deterioration, of danger, of impotence. He actually suffers loss of power by it. The effect of ugliness can be measured by the dynamometer. Whenever man is depressed, he has a sense of the proximity of something ugly. His sense of power, his will to power, his courage, his pride—they decrease with the ugly, they increase with the beautiful." All his words have been confirmed by the more solemn, if no more convincing, studies of Ph.D's. But to date there has not been any study of the relation of physical monotony and positive squalor to crime, nor of the subconscious effect upon civic pride of mere loveliness of environment. Until some such cachet of alleged statistical indicativeness is forthcoming, the sneers will probably continue. Certainly to date, the only thought given to the esthetics of planning, aside from a few planners who never admit to it verbally unless it be to their wives in the dark of night, is by architects designing monuments to themselves with government money or by government housing authorities successfully trying to suppress it in the name of economy and efficiency. When a beautiful parkway or an esthetically satisfying subdivision comes into being, ninety-nine times out of a hundred it is, as the movies say, purely coincidental.

The purposeful esthetic qualities of medieval towns have been described by Camillo Sitte; every traveler is aware of them, and calls them "picturesque," mistakenly. The Piazza San Marco, the Plaza Major of Salamanca, the Places de la Cathèdrale of innumerable French towns—Albi, Bourges, Chartres—the market places of England and Belgium, these are deliberate, dynamic designs. And later, when cannon opened the grand avenues and the Renaissance brought back the concept of static symmetry, the great axial plans opened on a mountain, the sea, a fine colonnade or building, or groups of buildings, or else when long and extended the avenue itself became the view, the trees closing in always beyond, until at the end of long travel a turn or a closure of permanency brought it to an end. The minor axes were carefully proportioned, and the buildings were meticulously studied for placing, form and height. In other words, it was three-dimensional and consequently architectural planning. In typical gridiron planning the axis has degenerated into a series of parallel lines without emphasis, leading to a garbage dump, a slum, or an empty space.

This does not mean one must have either the "grand plan" or the sinusoidal street. It merely means taking care and thought in relation to topography: giving variety in the type and size of street, whether arterial highway, business thoroughfare, straight or curved or dead-end residential street; seeing that there is uniformity of architecture and planting within the confines of each, permitting variation from street to street; that open places and public structures are placed with an eye for their effect on their surroundings and each other. It means, above all, three-dimensional thinking. The ground plan of a city, no matter how fine, is completely meaningless to the person walking through it unless it is also expressed in the third dimension. The ground plan controls only the great general movements of people and things; the particular development of the particular street or square is what

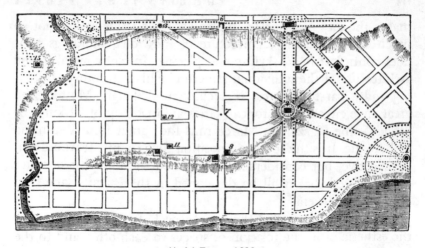

Model Town—1830

Legend: 1 Public green, with fountain in center. 2 Town house. 3 Church. 4 Small public building. 5 Large public building. 6 Arch. 7 Fountain. 8 Bank. 9 Church. 10 Church. 11 Bank. 12 Church. 13 Pillar or obelisk. 14 Public burying ground. 15 Handsome dwelling, or public monument. 16 Pillar or obelisk. N. B. The dots represent trees.

"Some of the streets it will be observed are wider than others, a circumstance which builders, on account of their varied means, will find an advantage. Some persons prefer building or living in narrow and retired streets; others seek those more public and open to observation. In this plan, I think regularity will be found combined with variety, simplicity with beauty, and symmetry with a sufficient attention to the multifarious circumstances of man. There is scarcely a street in it that does not present some handsome object to the view: there is scarcely a turn that will not surprise us with something unexpected, and it is at the same time of such a character as to be accommodated to the circumstances of almost every town in our country.

"The spots marked 3, 4, 8, 9, 10, 11, and 12, I have reserved for public buildings, churches, banks, and the like. I say reserved, and the word is meant to have a meaning beyond a paper plan. Such edifices are always expected to be ornamental to a city, and the public complain when they are not so. The public act justly, but those who build them have also a right to expect something from the public. Duties are always reciprocal. If the public wish societies to erect handsome edifices, it should give them ground that will show these edifices to advantage; not compel them to build, as it very often does, in lanes, and amid the very vilest tenements in the city. All this may easily be effected, by reserving ground at the first laying out of our towns. Let this be done: let the public then at proper times offer these desirable situations to those societies or companies that will improve them most, and architecture will take a start among us, of which we can now scarcely conceive. Cherished, it will labor hard for us in return; our cities will be ornamented; our towns will follow, and the land will become beautiful as it is blessed."

"Architecture in the United States," 1830.

makes the city pleasant or unpleasant,[12] and this means not so much control of the architecture of individual buildings as it does control of bulk, skyline and placing. In fact control of the architecture of the individual structure is likely to prove stultifying and a bar to progress in architectural design. Most of the great civic effects of European cities are made up of all kinds of "styles"—the Piazza San Marco runs the gamut from Byzantine to Baroque. It is the total composition that counts. It would still be effective, but considerably duller, had the local bankers and FHA insisted that it all be developed in the Italian Cape Cod current in their era.

It must become part of the social aspect of city replanning that the esthetic of it, the relation of spaces to each other and to the buildings that form the spaces, is admitted to be as important to health and welfare as sewers and playgrounds.[13]

Another important sociological aspect of city replanning is the declining population curve, and the still greater drop in the fertility rate. It is a truism that historically no great city has been self-regenerating. When the great balance of population was rural, this did not matter particularly, as there were ample reserves for the cities to draw upon. Today the situation is different. From 1900, when the ratio was 60% rural and 40% urban, the picture has changed until in 1940 the ratio was 43.5% rural and 56.5% urban. The cities can no longer depend on the country as a reservoir of population. But the cities still show a family size that is far below the reproduction rate needed to maintain either themselves or the nation, and because the balance of population has shifted from country to city the nation itself, and not just the cities, becomes endangered. The more urban areas, as a whole, grow at the expense of rural areas, the greater the danger gets to be. And yet, because the urban family size is, on the average, less than four persons, and consequently

[12] See *Town Planning* by Thomas Sharp (Pelican Books) particularly pages 102-108. This booklet is one of the best on town planning for the general reader.

[13] Incidentally, why are all city playgrounds so drear and bleak, so bald, woebegone and desolate? They are as bare and functional as the inside of a toilet bowl.

the largest market demand is, momentarily, for dwelling units of not more than two bedrooms, large scale government and private enterprise refuse to build accommodations for a higher average. This will ultimately have disastrous effects upon the central city —is having them now, as this too contributes to the exodus to periphery and suburb by those families that do have children. What it means in terms of the number of children can be seen from the school statistics of New York City. In 1936 there were 1,127,361 pupils; 716,957 elementary, 126,498 junior high, 285,-906 high school. In 1943 there were 525,136 elementary, 144,895 junior high, 242,909 high school,—a total of 912,940, or a total loss of 214,421 pupils in seven years.[14]

Nationally, there has been in the last ten years a decline of 12.5% in the population under 15 years of age in 1,077 cities of 10,000 population or more. The population between the ages of 55 and 70 has increased 36.5%. For the cities, 92 of them, of more than 100,000 the figures are: *United States*, total population, +4.5%; *92 cities*: under 5 years, −14.9%; 5-9 years, −20.9%; 10-14 years, −4.6%; 55-59 years, +32.5%; 60-64 years, + 31.4%; 65-69 years, + 53.1%.[15]

It may be, of course, that not even building-in a satisfactory environment will save the cities and the nation from a drastic decline in population. The trend may be part of a long biological swing due to unknown causes, or it may be due to artificial biological factors inherent in the nervous tension of urban living. Enid Charles and other population experts are convinced it is the latter, plus of course the economic problem of rearing children decently in the city in the face of what Frederick L. Ackerman has called "highly organized discomfort." The blithe way in which this impending danger is ignored by all public officials is really amazing.

It is nothing short of startling that an institution such as the Metropolitan Life Insurance Company should in all seriousness

[14] *All the Children*. 44th Report of the Superintendent of Schools, City of New York.

[15] "Urban Population Trends and the Public Schools," Fred. A. Conrad University of Arizona in *The Elementary School Journal*; and 16th U. S. Census.

propose an enormous development based on an average family size of 2.75 persons, providing only some 400 units with more than two bedrooms out of a total of 12,000 apartments! And it is no less startling that because of Congressional limitations on the cost per room per dwelling unit, USHA was forced to build far more units for the small family than for the large families for whom private enterprise is building less and less. No wonder there is an exodus to the suburbs, for the number of bedrooms in the small homes built in subdivisions average 2.7, and the families who can afford them naturally move into them.

Clearly, an essential part of the city of the future must be the provision of shelter for adequate family life as well as the creation of an environment suitable for child raising.[16]

[16] Cleveland Rodgers in *New York Plans for the Future* has written of this ably and at length.

5. EFFORTS

THE FINANCIAL AND PHYSICAL PLIGHT OF THE CITIES WAS NOT
generally realized by the general public or even by municipal
officials until the advent of the Depression. The expensive
Twenties showed strains and plaster cracks, but they were lightly
papered over with stock certificates. The peak was reached when
the mooring mast atop the Empire State Building was finally
completed and a Goodyear blimp flew symbolically around it.
Nothing, it seemed even then, could go higher or be more useless than that stainless steel monument to financial vanity—
something had to come down.

When the collapse came, the cities found themselves facing
bankruptcy, physical decay, industrial stagnation, and social collapse. The government set up rescue agencies, among them the
Public Works Administration, the Federal Housing Administration, the Civil Works Administration, (later the Works
Progress Administration) and the Home Owners' Loan Corporation. They had to move quickly, there was no time for over-all
planning, and in spite of the years of hullabaloo about city
planning, there were no over-all plans. Construction programs
were pushed regardless, out of dire necessity. People had to be
put to work, and the construction industry was a basic one,
which stimulated production in all sorts of manufacturing fields.
Schools, roads, sewage disposal plants, housing projects, civic

buildings were put into work with only the sketchiest regard for location, future development of the city or, indeed, anything except the need for employment, the need to give the country a shot in the arm. Much of the money was actual federal grant, the balance large federal loans at low rates of interest and long term amortization.

Cities which had formerly been so afflicted with civic ophthalmia that, like Washington and Buffalo, they never saw the foul hovels in the very shadow of the Capitol or the City Hall, suddenly became conscious of slums, blight and general decay, Robert D. Kohn, who toured the country as head of the Housing Division of the PWA, remarked that whereas formerly reception committees used carefully to steer the visitor up the main stem so as to point with pride at the homes of local millionaires, they now instead took him around to the mud and ruts of the shanty towns and Hoovervilles and boasted of the extent of their slums and the number of outdoor privies. Two-thirds of a nation found where the other third lived because by exploiting their existing slums they could dip into the federal pot.

The Civil Works Administration was used, among other urgent, necessary but heretofore neglected things, to make a Real Property Inventory. It revealed shocking conditions, so shocking that the most elementary kind of civic stock-taking, had there ever been any, would have revealed them. Our cities had simply never rebuilt themselves. They were leprous, like a living organism that had ceased to renew its tissue.

The Home Loan Bank took over mortgages, and could have taken title to half our urban centers. Home ownership, recklessly promoted by irresponsible speculators and abetted by irresponsible lending institutions, exploded in the pants pockets of the poor and the near poor who had been persuaded that they "owned" a home, when they really owed one. Expansion, high construction costs, high land costs, high finance had broken down the fine old ideal of a home "free and clear." Whereas people had formerly borrowed money to pay for a home, now they borrowed a home while they paid for the money.[1]

Nor was this fiction of "ownership" limited to homes. Loans of over one hundred percent had been made on great office buildings, hotels, and apartments, and the "bonds" sold promiscuously to whatever widows and children had held out on Wall Street. The ostensible owners had no "equity" whatever in many of these ventures, the "security" behind the bond was a mass of building material which even in good times could not earn enough to pay interest, and which in bad times could not even be sold. None of the great institutions investing in real estate had ever set up any reserves, nor had trusts, estates, mortgage-holders or private owners. They took income tax "depreciation," but happy in the thought that the land would always increase in value faster than the structure deteriorated, they milked the profits out without regard for a day of reckoning. In 1872 property at the corner of Main and Main was worth only fifty cents a square foot, and in 1902 it was "worth" four dollars. So in 1932 it was—or wasn't it?—going to be worth seven.

It wasn't.

While the HOLC was rescuing distressed home owners and lending institutions, the Federal Housing Administration was proceeding with its program of stimulating the house-building industry. To accomplish this it had to set up objectives directly opposed to many of those of the HOLC. In order to get construction going FHA went about guaranteeing the principal of the mortgage to banks in return for lower interest rates and a long-term amortized mortgage. The HOLC naturally wanted high rates of interest and short term mortgages, as more profit-

---

[1] "It (the HOLC) acquired over a million mortgages, representing about 18% of the total mortgaged home owners in the United States, but even so, the mortgages accepted for refinancing amounted to only 34% of those who applied. Furthermore, by the end of the decade the HOLC was forced to foreclose on about one-sixth of the mortgages accepted. The inability of this agency to rescue hundreds of thousands of home owners who needed help indicates the extremes to which home ownership had gone in the 1920's under encouragement from Government and business."

—John P. Dean, *Home Ownership, Is It Sound?*, Harper's, 1945.

able to the lending institutions. Neither agency exhibited any direct interest in the consumer. The policies of FHA, however, had many considerable indirect influences on him. Not only were interest rates lowered and the term of the mortgage extended, thus lowering carrying charges, but the amount of the loan was increased to 80 per cent, which eliminated one of the worst abuses of the old system, the second mortgage. The whole financial set-up was simplified, and the single monthly payment which included interest, amortization, taxes and insurance— "pay like rent"—had great appeal. The wisdom of the long-term mortgage remains to be proven, however. Ernest M. Fisher has —perhaps sardonically—observed "One of the fundamental tests of the soundness of any home financing program is whether it facilitates the payment of indebtedness. To be sound it must promote the liquidation, not perpetuation of debt." [2]

In order to minimize the risk involved in insuring loans, the FHA found it had to set up standards of site selection, site planning and construction. With a government guarantee taking the risk out of "risk capital," neither the lending institutions nor the builders would give a hoot about the quality of what was constructed unless forced to do so. One of the characteristics of the building industry, particularly the home-building portion of it, was its complete reliance on *caveat emptor*. Once title passed, the buyer had no recourse, no matter how bad the product, and only rarely was the builder either able or willing to stand back of it. Real estate laws were always framed to protect the financial interest of the lender, never the purchaser. Therefore, the positive standards of FHA acted in the nature of an assurance to the purchaser that the house met at least minimum standards of sound construction, and that the site planning incorporated necessary utilities as well as certain elements of good lay-out, such as separated traffic, larger blocks, parks, play-spaces, and often community facilities for the more isolated develop-

[2] In a speech to the National Conference on Post-War Housing, Chicago, March 9, 1944.

ments. The worst features of speculative sub-division promotion were eliminated from "FHA insured" projects,—a slogan that began to have real meaning to the buyers of small homes.[3]

The essence of FHA policy was to reach the largest possible market, the "lower middle class" as it is sometimes called, which is perfectly sound economically but still unable generally to afford accommodations in new dwellings in the center of the larger cities or in the denser portions of metropolitan areas. Almost all FHA developments, whether for sale or rent, therefore, were suburban or peripheral, since they had to be on cheap land. This, of course, added to the trend towards decentralization, and by siphoning still more people to outlying land did much to increase blight and to further endanger the value of mortgages in the older parts of cities.

At this same time the Housing Division of the Public Works Administration went into the large-scale housing field, trying first to reach the same market as FHA reached later, through assistance to private enterprise limited-dividend companies. This type of financing had a successful record in New York City under the supervision of the State Board of Housing, although the number of projects was small and none had been attempted outside the city. The PWA effort along these lines was unsuccessful, for there was so much chicanery and fancy-business in most of the set-ups, usually in an effort to palm off worthless land, that the attempt to operate in this field was given up. Only a very few of these projects were approved and built. Instead, PWA gave the country its first real low-rent public housing projects.

These projects were widely criticized, but although they did cost too much, for various reasons, they embodied sound principles: the subsidy was largely in the form of a capital grant;

[3] For a full and exceptionally clear statement of home-building and home-owners problems see *American Housing*, by Miles L. Colean et al, Twentieth Century Fund, 1944. Also, *Home Ownership, Is It Sound?*, by John P. Dean, Harper's, 1945; *Neighborhood Design & Control; an analysis of Planned Communities*, by Henry S. Churchill, The National Committee on Housing, 1944.

superblock planning was developed; the buildings were walk-ups; the coverage was low; the density was moderate; the interior planning provided rooms that were reasonably generous in size and livable in arrangement.

By 1937 there was enough interest in public housing for the creation of the United States Housing Authority, now the Federal Public Housing Authority. This authority was entrusted with a program of slum clearance and provision of "decent, safe and sanitary dwellings" for the economic lowest third of the nation. It was, therefore, directly concerned with the problems of the cities. Rural slums were the province of the Resettlement Administration.

USHA found itself with a mandate to clear slums, either by direct demolition on the site or by "equivalent elimination," i.e., the municipality was required, through its police power, to vacate and close, or to demolish or to repair, as many dwelling units as the Authority, acting through an agency called "the Local Authority," would build. Thus it added nothing to the sum-total of dwellings in the country. It also found itself faced with the old dilemma of land "values." In most instances it chose to build on vacant or semi-vacant land on the periphery; in a few instances, notably in New York City, it built on moderately close-in land and resorted to high densities to take up the land cost. In either case, whatever its choice, the result was a further extension of blight, either by direct depletion of population in the central areas or by putting a very much higher concentration of population on a limited site. This was rationalized to the socially minded on the one hand by claiming it brought down future land values and rents, allowing for cheaper purchase prices in the future and lower rents in the present, and to the real estate interests and municipal economists on the other by claiming it increased land values in the neighborhood of the project and reduced the costs of policing and health services.

The USHA program did provide decent, sanitary dwellings for a limited number of slum dwellers, but it did not approach a solution of the housing and slum clearance problem, and city planning received no more than lip service. It is characteristic of the confusion of purpose and the conflict of interests that USHA has been most furiously attacked for its failure to "solve" these problems by the very groups which have been most active in preventing the Congress from making sufficient appropriations to carry out a long range, far-sighted program. USHA did spread throughout the country the idea of the superblock and the beginning of thinking in terms of neighborhood planning. It failed, notoriously, to integrate the projects either with any general plan for the city or with the character of existing neighborhoods. Stereotyped monotony was enforced from Washington in the name of economy. Although costs, compared with World War I housing, comparable private enterprise housing, or the PWA early projects, were astonishingly low and the quality of construction was good, the visual results which last long after the cost is forgotten are deplorable. Completely out of scale with surrounding structures, dull and spiritless in design, they range from coast to coast, recognizable at a glance as the dwellings of the deserving poor. There are, of course, some exceptions, but these were due mostly to the action of vigorous Local Authorities and recalcitrant architects, with guts enough to resist the pressure from Washington. The great majority, however, could not stand up against the demand for economy at any cost. The statistical and double-entry approach was used exclusively, and no dalliance with such abstractions as visual satisfaction were permitted to interfere.

Thus both public and private large-scale housing under government auspices contributed to the increase of blight, and did little or nothing to help the cities solve any essential difficulties. Both ends were played against the middle, nothing was clear cut in the economic policy, and as a consequence no real planning was possible.

The prejudice against *planning* in whatever guise persisted in spite of the obvious confusion and error that lack of it made manifest. Politicians and private enterprise would have none of it and kept it out of the cities. There was some planning on the national level, but it was within the various agencies. Chief among these was the National Resources Planning Board, which did some magnificent research work into the resources, physical and human, of the country, and did a tremendous job of organizing and stimulating regional and state planning. As long as it stuck to research and stimulation it was tolerated, but when it finally ventured to produce an actual plan for social security, Congress killed it. In the field of urban planning a whole series of its reports form an essential part of the basic ground-work for all future effort.[4]

The NRPB also issued a series of pamphlets, digests of its larger reports, for popular consumption, and its regional offices did much excellent work in popularizing the idea of local planning, so that its influence was felt everywhere.

The Federal Housing Administration, the Federal Reserve Bank, the Home Owners Loan Corporation, and Farm Securities Administration (formerly the Resettlement Administration) also made studies relating to their particular interest in urbanism or housing. These were all well worth while, exploring as they did various facets of a complex subject. But they were not pulled together so that a complete and coherent policy could be set up, and they were so technical as to be of interest only to professionals and did not reach the layman.

This chaotic condition was slightly ameliorated when the President, by executive order, consolidated some sixteen agencies concerned with housing under the National Housing Agency. This, however, is a war agency, and consequently has not been able to get to work on any full-scale program of research in housing and urbanism, although a start has been made. What is needed, of course, is a technical research and fact-gathering division which will make available to the interested public all the vast experience of the various departments of government in building, equipment and management. This should be a

<hr>

[4] Principally: *Our Cities, their role in the National Economy; Urban Planning and Land Problems; Problems of a Changing Population.*

service to the public and not, like the Bureau of Standards, merely a service to the producer.

On the purely local level, virtually no planning was done. The United States Housing Act of 1937 authorized the creation of Local Authorities under State enabling acts. These were run by volunteer unpaid public-minded citizens; funds derived from the loans for projects paid for clerical and technical staffs. No provision was made for financing long-range or comprehensive planning. New York City was more fortunate than most places. It had a huge reservoir of condemned-as-unsafe buildings, and it made deals with owners to have the buildings wrecked by WPA (relief) workers, thus saving the owners taxes, and from the sale of salvage was able to finance some research and study. The Mayor's Committee on City Planning also used the WPA, and did some very essential basic research and mapping of city conditions, supplementing the work of the Real Property Inventory.

In other cities, particularly the medium sized ones, it was almost impossible for the Local Authority to do more than plan its immediate project. Exceptionally, a far sighted and forceful executive director would be able to enlist some support, public or private, for studies of one kind or another, but at best these were limited in scope and sporadic in nature.

It would seem essential, in the near future, to make Local Housing Authorities part of the municipal administration, as paid Commissioners. It is absurd that large public funds, often running into tens of millions of dollars, and more important still, that policies affecting large numbers of citizens, perhaps as many as twenty-five thousand or more, should be left in the hands of an unpaid part time body, no matter how able and civic-minded its members. Such conversion into a component part of the city government has ample precedent in the similar development of school, health and library boards from extra-municipal agencies into city departments directly responsible to the Mayor and to the public.

The same lack of funds which hampered Housing Authorities hamstrung the City Planning Commissions. Most of them were moribund anyway, and those that were active were powerless from lack of public support and consequently lack of money. The efforts of the NRPB and the USHA did a good deal to revive the interest of City Councils in their Planning Commissions, and the new charter of New York provided for a well-paid, quasi-independent Commission with wide powers and strong directives. For various reasons it has accomplished little to date beyond the routine duties, and its independence has been undermined. The Chicago Plan Commission, however, is doing a remarkably effective job. The haussmannism of the Burnham Plan is giving way before a series of intensive studies of neighborhoods and changing industrial conditions. It remains to be seen whether these studies, which are unimposing but really vital to the welfare of the city, will result in as much accomplishment as the spectacular plans for the reclamation of the lake front.

Los Angeles too has made valuable contributions to the technique of neighborhood organization within the framework of the city's disorganization.

Many smaller cities are also allowing their Commissions to make studies and paper plans. Some of these are excellent in their analysis, many are comprehensive in their surveys and factual data. A few also give consideration to the problems of the people and of the city as a place in which to live. Whether any serious action will be taken on any of these plans depends on the development of a favorable economic and social climate. If there is a speculative land and housing boom, probably nothing will be done, since any action that is favorable to the public welfare and that requires controls is inimical to speculation.

Some of the smaller cities are trying the administrative experiment of tying together various agencies, such as the Housing Authority, Planning Commission, and perhaps the County or Regional Planning Board, by means of "interlocking directorates." The executive director of one may be chairman of another, or even in some cases executive director of both. Cleveland, Syracuse, Louisville, and a good many other places are trying this in various degrees.

Thus, if the multiplication of drawings for the rebuilding of cities and the reclamation of run-down areas is any indication, the concept of physical planning is making slow but definite headway. Progress in economic planning, and in the legal and cultural adjustments that must accompany, if not precede, the economic planning, has not, as previously discussed, kept pace with the techniques of physical planning.

We have yet to reconcile in our thinking, and consequently in political action, public effort and private enterprise.

We have yet to subordinate immediate private gain to public interest and long-range private benefit.

We have yet, in the broad field of physical planning, to establish workable objectives which are neither so limited by immediate compromise as to be nearly worthless if not, indeed, harmful, nor so far outside the present framework of society as to be doubtful of even eventual accomplishment.

Whatever these objectives turn out to be—and they are in process of being worked out, the fat from some of the heads is being clarified—the mechanical pivot on which they revolve is the firm control of land-use in a democratic society.

It may be worthwhile to briefly consider the first two notions before going on to the third, which will be the subject of the last chapter.

The conflict between what are called public endeavor and private enterprise is, in any large-scale venture, mostly semantics. As soon as any enterprise involves scores of millions of dollars and effects the living of thousands of persons, it becomes affected with the public interest; often it becomes involved in public, or quasi-public financing.

In slum-clearance, "urban rehabilitation," large-scale housing, the line between public endeavor and private enterprise virtually disappears. Public work employs funds derived from the public at large, by taxation or by the issuance of bonds which are bought by the public and on which interest and amortization are paid for through taxes or out of rents. Private enterprise employs funds taken from the public-almost-as-large by the building up of excess profits into surplus which must be disgorged, by the return on investments of "sacred trustee funds" deposited in banks or insurance companies by the public, by the direct employment of such funds, or by the sale of mortgage "bonds." In any event, the money comes from thousands of little people. Both public and private enterprise employ private architects, engineers, and contractors. Both buy their materials from private supply houses and private manufacturers. Both seek labor in the same market. Both pay off the cost of their enterprise out of rents, that is, the public pays for it. "Low-rent public housing," which serves a public unable to pay an economic rent, is the recipient of a direct and acknowledged subsidy. "Limited dividend" housing, paying a limited return because of limited rents, is the recipient of a subsidy in the form of partial tax exemption. The proponents of large-scale urban redevelopment, the associations of small-fry builders, unite to demand subsidy in the form of the power of eminent domain, of write-off on land cost, of release from the obligation to pay decent wages or do decent planning. They have found a new slogan: The American Way of Public Subsidy for Private Enterprise.

Now there is nothing wrong with public subsidy for large scale enterprise, and it is the American Way, or one of the Ways, and has been from the days of Alexander Hamilton. It is only when private enterprise refuses the obligations, duties and control that go with the public interest that subsidy becomes an evil thing.

Nor is this essential similarity of public and private large scale enterprise solely a matter of economics. For instance, the control over tenants' living, what is called "regimentation" in public projects, is as strict in Parkchester as it is in Queensbridge Houses, the regulations in force in Baldwin Hills Village are as pernickety as those in Ramona Gardens.

Thus the confusion, in the field of urban planning, that exists between private enterprise and public endeavor, boils down to the old battle, long since fought out in the fields of transportation and communication for instance, of subordination of immediate private gain to public interest and stabilized instead of speculative private benefit. The railroads, bus companies, telephone, telegraph and radio (all of them private enterprise), have all eventually had to submit to public control in order to safeguard the public. Large scale private housing will, sooner or later, be forced into doing likewise and for the same reasons.

The great English report on land use and control, known as the Uthwatt Report,[5] states the case briefly thus:

> The fact that land is held by large numbers of owners whose individual interests lie in putting their own particular piece of land to the most particular use for which they can find a market, whereas the need of the State and the community is to ensure the best use of all land irrespective of financial return. If planning is a necessity and an advantage to the community, as is undoubtedly the case, a means must be found for removing the conflict between private and public interest.

Like More's Utopia, this is dust around the corner.

[5] *Expert Committee on Compensation and Betterment.* The Hon. Mr. Justice Uthwatt, Chairman, Sec. 37, (b) (ii). Ministry of Works and Planning.

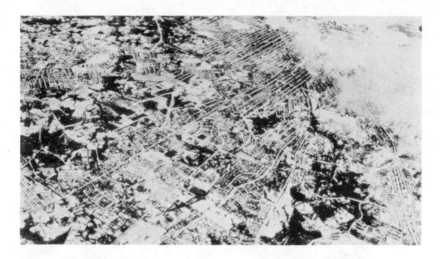

The confusion of industry and living—the fringes of a great city.

A typical small town. Note the paradox of ample land and huddled houses. Vacant lots and narrow frontages, undifferentiated street pattern. Contrast this with the photograph of Litchfield, with the Los Angeles redevelopment proposal.

"Sprouted gables and turrets"

Three story apartments with "courts" between. No light, no air, no form—unending drabness—stretching from Brooklyn to San Francisco.

A typical attempt to achieve variety, ghastly in its result. Have you ever really looked at it?

"SOCIETY AS A WHOLE . . .
IS MAINLY RESPONSIBLE . . ."

A substantial street—the houses are not beautiful, but the place is pleasant.

The monotony of uniformity, the endless street. You walk down it often.

"AND SOCIETY AS WHOLE . . . SHOULD PAY THE COST"

Blight. It is next door to you.

Those who could moved to the suburbs, leaving this behind for you to do something about.

Planlessness: A new subdivision—unpaved, treeless and forlorn; mortgaged to the hilt, but Home. On the fringes of your city.

Dignity in decay. These row houses are 60 years old. It is the environment that has gone bad, not the houses.

"La Ville Radieuse"—Chicago version.

136

Chicago. The Burnham Plan. "The paper architectural development of a civic center."

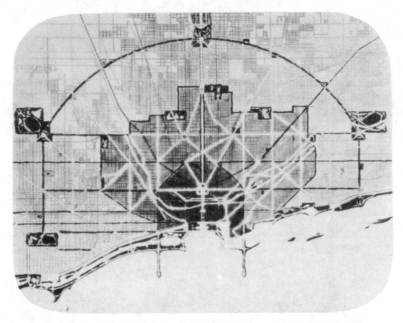

Chicago. The Burnham Plan, 1909. Concept, not statistic

FUTURE PLANNING
AREAS OF CHICAGO

TO BE REBUILT

RIPE FOR REBUILDING

FOR CONSERVATION

FOR NEW GROWTH

NON RESIDENTIAL

NORTH BRANCH

STATE
STREET

MADISON
STREET

CHICAGO RIVER

SOUTH BRANCH

LAKE MICHIGAN

CAL CREEK

CANAL

COOK COUNTY

LAKE CALUMET

WOLF LAKE

ILLINOIS

INDIANA

This shows what needs to be done, the question is how to do it. 1944.

138

Not the heart but the viscera. The endless slums of our cities.

Main Street anywhere.

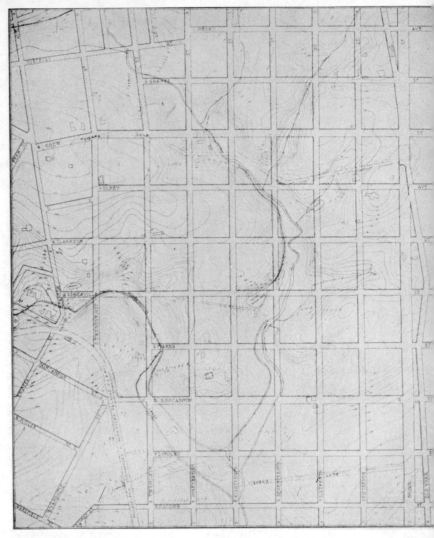

"City Planning, Philadelphia, 1871: A gridiron street system, planned for a hilly river gorge, without regard for topography or the varying traffic needs of different streets. No effective use is planned for the stream banks; some of the streets could not possibly be built."

"The Same Area Replanned, 1925: the street plan has been adjusted to the topography; main thoroughfares have been differentiated by location and design. Provision is made for river bank parks and public institutions; the area has been zoned to protect the plan."

Old neighborhoods used as the nuclei for now communities.

143

Fantasia. The Pentagon, Washington, D. C. "One thing that happens when a building for 40,000 people is put up, appears in the model photograph: a fantastic network of roads, cloverleafs, underpasses and overpasses. This influence is not confined to the site, generous as the 400-acre site happens to be. For miles around the results of building the Pentagon are visible: the reclaimed slums, the broad roads, and the new, integrated approaches to the capital. Perhaps the greatest lesson of the Pentagon is here: as building approaches the scale technically feasible, the distinction between architecture and city planning vanishes. Despite its shortcomings, the Pentagon gives a real foretaste of the future."

Chatham Village

Baldwin Hills Village

Queensbridge Houses, New York City. Site plan. A city "superblock" plan—six large blocks instead of twelve. Six story apartments, shopping center, community building, nursery school, in-block playgrounds. 12,000 people, all of one economic level. W. F. R. Ballard, Henry S. Churchill, Frederick G. Frost, Burnett Turner, architects.

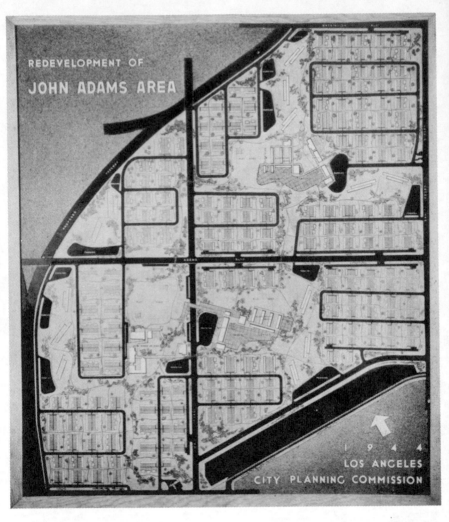

The new approach—the integrated community within the city. Main traffic flows around, primary access is separated from local roads serving residences only. There are single family, row and apartment units. Schools (including junior high school), recreation and community facilities are easily and safely reached. Light industry is right at hand. The pattern of the future is beginning to evolve.

6. TRENDS

WE SEE OUR CITIES, GREAT AND SMALL, FALLING apart, disintegrating. We talk a great deal about replanning them. But if the only changes which our "replanning" can bring about are ones which will leave things the same, there is little use. For one thing, we have never really answered the question, what kind of a city are we planning for?

Planning cities in a changing world is not an *ad hoc* process. There are inevitable forces of technological change at work which will bring economic and social changes in their wake. These forces will condition our city plans. The issue is whether or not we will vainly try to ignore these forces or whether we will try to build our cities around them.

Planning presumably is the expression of man's will to order. There must be a frame of reference, physical and mental, for the ordinary procedures of living; this frame must be recognizable, and it must allow reasonable freedom of action within its limits. The limits are set by society as a whole, and all planning, if it is to be effectuated, must take place within those limits. They are, however, larger and more flexible than the scared conservative thinks they are.

How will the city of the future differ from the city of today and yesterday, if at all, and why? What are the pressures for change which those intrusted with planning should bear in mind?

They are many and diverse. They come at the city planner from all sides, converging on his problem from every angle. It is not possible to say which are primary to his consideration, which secondary, for they mutually interact and no one is unaffected by all the others. Economic pressures are built up by technological changes, and these, in turn, permit new pressures, set up new social strains and stresses, and create unrest and demands for legal, political, and fiscal readjustments. These last three are always laggard, always conservative, far behind the business and industrial enterprise that, in our economy, is the keynote of the others. Essentially the law is the bulwark of the feeble and the frightened—though often perverted to the malfeasance of the strong—and political action can proceed only as fast as the electorate will allow. Fiscal policy is at the mercy of both law and politics. Planning, which in a democracy is essentially legal, political and fiscal, must therefore also proceed slowly.

At the risk of some repetition, it may be well to briefly particularize some of the forces and pressures mentioned. The more important are:

Developments in power source and distribution. The internal combustion engine changed transportation and gave us first the automobile and now the airplane. Wireless distribution of power may be next, or some form of atomic energy stemming from the use of high explosives or from electronics. Certainly the comparatively inefficient motor of today is not the last word.

Electric power changed manufacturing, both in regard to process and location. The vacuum tube and other developments in electronics are changing processes and communications. Inventions in physics, chemistry, and biochemistry may entirely alter the relationship of factory to raw material, and may develop new sources of cultivated raw materials—of which silk is an ancient, and soy bean and cotton are relatively new, examples—which will be as important as the mined raw materials. Increasing use of the light metals and of plastics will also make for industrial shifts. All of these developments tend in the direction of less space for manufacturing, less of a tie to any given location, fewer but more highly skilled operatives, more leisure.

The chemical discoveries in medicine will further cut the death rate and increase the life span. The consequences of this are of enormous importance, not only for this country and Europe, but also for Asia.

All of these trends and many others will make possible that dispersion of industrial and population concentration that the bombing plane and winged bomb have made imperative. Just as heavy artillery knocked down the walls of the city, so the high explosive bomb will scatter it. The technological processes, metallurgical, physical, and chemical that produced heavy artillery, changed trade and industry; the same process is taking place again. New methods of death and destruction are one with new methods of life and production.

The pressures set up by these forces will affect cities physically, socially, and economically on different levels.

On the first, or international level, air transportation and the new markets opened by it will establish new trade routes and trans-shipment centers, and will pass over some now existing. That you "fly north to get to the east," is something that must be kept in mind. Trade with the Orient and India will surely increase, and the trend of trade in this country will be westward. The consequences of the peace will be reflected quite specifically in the growth and nature of our cities.

On the national level it is probable that manufacturing will seek, in general, locations that relate to market rather than to raw material, and that can provide ample facilities for motor transportation both by land and air. There has already been a considerable break from concentrated manufacturing centers, with their multi-story factories and warehouses, congested streets, high taxes and complicated building laws, to outlying areas where it is possible to build one-story plants with great parking fields. New sources of power, whatever they may be, will stimulate this. Inevitably, this will affect the residential pattern of communities also. The eventual effects of what is called "regional planning" or "geo-planning" will be of great importance. TVA is the first example of what geo-technics can do. There is not the slightest doubt about the tremendous possibilities of this over-all approach: TVA is there for those who have eyes to see; David E. Lilienthal's book, *TVA—Democracy on the March*, should be read by everyone. It is a confirmation of the soundness of democracy and of the possibility of democratic planning procedures. Beyond TVA lie the agricultural riches and power released by Boulder Dam and the Bonneville Dam, the opening of new mineral resources in the Rockies, the replanning possibilities of the old valleys of the Connecticut and the Delaware, the realization of the vast potentials of the great rivers of the middle plain.

The local level is what concerns us, who are concerned with city planning, most of all. The national and international pressures will be slow but pitiless, they must be constantly kept in mind in relation to any specific city. The local pressures are with us now and at once. They provide the criteria and objectives which planners must work for.

The centrifugal population shift in metropolitan areas will almost certainly continue. Two primary forces are working here: one is the shift in industrial location already mentioned, and population follows industry; the other is a continuation of the vastly increased amount of land made available by modern means of transportation and the vastly increased economic ability of people to take advantage of it. The economic "surplus" which in predominantly rural economies was once the characteristic of cities, is no longer a monopoly of intensive concentrations of population. The produce of this surplus, leisure, and the cultural developments that leisure both creates and consumes, also is no longer a monopoly of such concentrations, and will become less so. Books, the movies, radio, and television, all lessen dependence on the central city; improved transportation in the future may make it clear that perhaps the Metropolitan Museum could serve more people better in, let us say White Plains; or that Forty-second Street and Broadway could draw on a larger and more cosmopolitan audience in Denver, Colorado. This is surely exaggeration to point the moral, for there are still, and always will be, those who like crowds and the closeness of their kind, but it is no exaggeration to foresee the development of a great number of cultural centers not located in central cities, and drawing on large regions for their support.

The other side to this is that the cities may retain their essential cultural elements such as museums, spectacles, scientific libraries, universities, and so on, together with concentrations of retail trade and "business" as distinct from large industry. They would thus return to their original function of market places for the exchange of goods and ideas. It is noteworthy that already over 50 per cent of the gainfully employed in the major cities earn their living in the "service industries"—white collar workers, clerks in stores, garage mechanics, waiters, taxi and bus drivers, laundries, and all the allied types of "non-productive" work.

It is quite lkely that this trend may be strengthened by the changing age-composition of the population already referred to. An older population requires different things from what younger people require in the way of activities and service. They are less inclined to industrial work, industry is less inclined to want them. Their children will have left them, and they will be attracted to the companionship of city crowds, the cultural opportunities and the comparative ease of living. Their children will live in the region, to be near work and to be able to raise *their* children decently. It would seem that the proportion of older people living in cities will greatly increase over what it is now.

The increased maturity of city dwellers and their increased leisure, the emphasis on more mature cultural interests that this implies, should have a direct effect on the esthetics of city planning. The appreciation of architecture and spacial relationships is in a large measure a question of tempo; if you are rushed mentally by the pressure of affairs, or physically by transportation, little is seen, and nothing registers, nothing matters. One does not realize how horrible our cities are until, some quiet morning, there is opportunity to walk leisurely to work. The old cities were always seen by people walking; as they walked, what they saw affected them deeply. Today we neither walk nor see nor care. Architecture cannot be satisfactory if there is no response, if cities are inhabited only by the blind, the careless, and the harassed.

Finally, there is the greatest of all centrifugal pressures—defense against warfare from the air. The destruction of cities in the present war is only a prelude to the destruction that will be possible in World War III. The only possible protection is scattering of industry, buildings, people. This is of a piece with the other forces making for decentralization. True, there are some "industrial designers" who foresee cities of tunnels and caves, air-conditioned, efficiently lighted, violet-rayed, sprayed with the faint nostalgic scent of automobile exhausts and pervaded by soft music and inspiring oratory from loud speakers. Inter-urban communication, when physically necessary, will be either by rocket planes into the carefully blacked-out empyrean, or by traveling a hundred miles an hour over express roads which will be completely enclosed by glass block and controlled by radar. Somehow, the dispersion pattern seems easier although less romantic.

It seems probable, in the light of the various forces at work, that the forms of cities may undergo radical changes which will be more far reaching in nature than any they have undergone in the long historical past. This will not, of course, be true for all cities, any more than it has been for many of the most ancient ones now still existing. There are cities which are many hundreds of years old which are virtually unchanged. People live and die in them and the daily routines of life go on much as they did when the world was new and all. Damascus comes to mind,

Bagdad, Cordoba, Stettin, Ghent, and Vilna. There are innumerable others all over the world, including the pueblos of the United States. Although life in its component parts goes on, the cities themselves are only half-alive, they survive as something outside the main current of world events. The technologies of their regions remain virtually unchanged from the ancient days, and they are still adequate to serve their ancient and original purposes of local trade. This is not true and cannot be true of cities whose reason for being is the industrial technology of the modern world. Nor is there any city so remote as to be outside the current of world war. They must change to meet the new facts that face them. What is so difficult, what makes adjustment so difficult and planning so imperative, is the rate of change. The world of flight and electronics is upon us, and there is little time for the honored process of evolution. Our future is a revolutionary one, and it must be planned revolution or it will be confusion, if not chaos.

There have been a good many attempts to reveal the form of the future city. Most of these have failed to take into consideration the persistence of the past or the tenacity of human habit. And yet since as Blake has said, "Everything possible to be believed is an image of truth," it will be well to pause and consider.

There is Le Corbusier's belief that life will be mechanized on a completely rational basis: "La Ville Radieuse," the stately rows of skyscrapers, the well-organized open spaces, the direct lines of communication, the de-humanizing of existence, the complete lack of humor characteristic of the authoritarian process. The Radiant City would be splendid and heartless, the lights Kleig lights, the radiance that of false dawn. Yet in part it is a viable concept—there is no reason why the skyscraper should be scrapped because it has been abused; it provides a way of life, and Le Corbusier has shown the possibilities of achieving it if anyone cares for it.

There is Frank Lloyd Wright's Broadacre City, the belief of a man who believes in democracy the way Jefferson believed in it. It roots back into the oldest American tradition—a house and a substantial piece of land for everyone who wants it. Privacy and neighborliness, elbow room and easy access to the communal needs and facilities, exquisite organization, beauty beyond our desert. Perhaps it is because he has expressed so clearly and simply the average American's dream that his concept has been so mocked by the high-priests. Yet it most surely is an image of truth, Keats' as well as Blake's.

Saarinen believes the city is an organic growth, that its cell structure has broken down but that it can be repaired if care is taken to follow biological precept in our planning. The analogy is false, an anthropomorphic concept. Cities live because of people, not the other way around. Yet there is much to be learned from the processes of nature if we are careful not to confuse that which is an organism with that which is humanly organized.

There are many lesser prophets paddling around, many of them with too much honor in their own country. Their beliefs are, for the most part, those of others, and the image of their truth is often merely a reflection.

It is not the purpose of this book to forecast form. Form follows function, as Louis Sullivan said, and the form may have many expressions. It does not concern us here whether the form of the tree that gives the shade is that of oak or maple or elm; the essential function with which we are concerned is the function of the city as a place in which people live. The outside forces—the soil, the climate, if you wish—have been described. There are, in addition, certain inherent qualities in the plant itself which can, at least partly, be recognized. The two together will, in time, determine the city's form.

The population of metropolitan areas will continue to increase, although the central cities probably will not, and may even decline.

In 1940 approximately 85 per cent of the total urban population of the United States lived in 140 metropolitan districts. The metropolitan districts of 1930 included 83 per cent of the urban population. Their population increase was somewhat greater than for the country as a whole. Between 1930 and 1940 the population in the central cities in the metropolitan areas increased by 6.1 per cent as compared to an increase of 16.9 per cent outside the central cities . . . Stating these figures another way, of the total metropolitan increase 54.3 percent occurred outside the central cities; the suburban areas grew 2.8 times as rapidly as the central cities, of which 35 actually declined between 1930 and 1940.[1]

The metropolitan areas, in other words, will tend to become more uniformly inhabited. The lines of growth have always been out from the center (of even small towns and villages) along the lines of best communication—railroads, inter-urban trolleys, main highways with bus lines, secondary highways by private cars. As the ownership of cars has increased, and bus lines have multiplied, the spaces between the older "mass transportation" routes have filled in. Factories are now locating in these "between route" areas, pulling more population to them, from the former centers. The three great industrial "flatlands" of northeastern New Jersey from the Hudson to the Raritan, of Buffalo—Lackawanna—Niagara Falls, and of Detroit, illustrate this process to a marked degree.

What is happening, therefore, is something different from the "satellite city" concept of Ebenezer Howard, or the "polynucleated city" of Lewis Mumford, although it is closer to the latter. The mesh of roads, factories, towns, shopping centers, ribbon developments, garbage dumps, railroads, air fields, and what not, is growing quite haphazardly and without regard for rational inter-communication, inter-dependent needs, or integrated function. Here and there are the old nuclei—Plainfield, Rahway, Montclair—Lackawanna, the Tonawandas—Dearborn, Flint.

These vast intermixed areas—the New York, Northeastern

[1] Lorin A. Thompson, in *Pencil Points*, April 1943.

New Jersey area comprises 2,514 square miles, the Detroit area, 746—make a great laboratory for the future urban pattern. Devastation from the air will be difficult for the industrial plants are widely scattered. What is needed is planned organization so that instead of being dreary and indeed foul wastelands, they will become fit areas in which to live, work and play.

The three districts already mentioned, together with Philadelphia—Chester, Chicago—Gary, Pittsburgh—Allegheny County—and a few smaller ones (Bridgeport, Ct. is one) present the most difficult problems, because of the objectionable nature of the basic heavy industries, with their smoke, fumes, stench, and industrial waste. They are also necessarily serviced by railroads, which add many difficulties. Still, it would be possible to make them in a large degree better. The great plants might be isolated in the center of open areas which could serve as parking fields, helicopter fields, and recreational fields, with no residence permitted nearer than a half-mile. The same would be true of the great automotive plants, which though not objectionable in themselves, are primary bombing targets. Bendix, N. J. and Willow Run, Mich., already present such a set-up. Smaller plants could be treated similarly, in groups, or even singly in wooded sections for better camouflage. The non-nuisance factories would not need such isolation and could well be scattered in the midst of the less densely built-up residential sections. Some of these have already been built in New Jersey, along U.S. 1, in the New Brunswick area, and no doubt elsewhere.

Some of the otherwise unusable land, such as that often occurring between railroads, might be intensively used for truck gardening, for the food problem for these metropolitan districts gets ever more acute. Freeways, such as the Pulaski Skyway, will have to be developed, and the employment-residence situation brought under control, if transportation is not to come to a complete impasse when normal use of automobiles is resumed. The freeways will have to be purposeful in their destination, not mere alleviations of a sector—the Pulaski Skyway for example is no good because it bottle-necks at both ends, and there is no relieving, or alternate route at either end to any place that is not a worse traffic jam than the bottle-neck. There is no reason why these freeways should not be built in strip parks, part of the recreational system of the area. TVA has already built such, and in heavy industrial sections they are essential.

The proper planning and control of these great industrial complexes is one of the most important planning jobs before us. It has not been given much thought, and presents grave difficulties. It is somewhat in the nature of regional planning, only it requires much tighter control than what is usually called regional planning. Control of any kind will be difficult because of the multitude of jurisdictions involved and the infinite feuds, jealousies, and hatreds of the office-holders. Even where there is co-operation, the legal complexities against mutual action remain. A long period of education will be necessary, and perhaps the over-riding force of imperative necessity, before much can be done. Nevertheless, without preliminary thought and study, it will be hard to take appropriate action at any time.

As the metropolitan areas are made more livable, the financial difficulties of the central cities will increase. The solution to the fiscal problem does not lie in the realm of physical city planning; cities will develop the way technological and social forces compel them; the fiscal problem will have to be solved concurrently, or at worst, ex post facto. "Urban redevelopment" simply cannot rebuild cities to present densities, because people won't continue to live in such discomfort unless they have no choice. To replan cities properly, densities must be reduced. And since, whether we admit it officially or not, taxes are a factor of total population earning capacity, our present real estate tax system makes no sense at all and puts the question of municipal finance right up to the tax experts. It is not a planning problem, because no matter how you plan the fiscal dilemma remains.

Actually, the cities face two great planning problems: how to restore livability and financial soundness to their cores; how to develop the peripheral land so as to maintain a sound balance with the centers and prevent over-expansion and undue neighborhood obsolescence.

Since peripheral land is cheap, and since the largest market is for medium and low-priced single family houses, building booms always produce the greatest volume of building—in terms of units, if not of costs—in such areas. Also, since previous booms have already subdivided much land, often wastefully, and there are consequently difficulties in the way of assemblage, re-platting, or the nature of the existing structures, the tendency is to go out beyond them. This is a perfectly natural thing for the developer to do, but it can hardly be called healthy from the point of view of the community at large.

The dilemma of urban center replanning has been mentioned. There has been emerging, in recent years, a theory of planning which has something of a common denominator for both urban redevelopment and peripheral expansion. This is the "neighborhood unit," which is much bruited about. The term has pretty well lacked definition, and is used indiscriminately for a *physical* neighborhood, a *social* neighborhood, a *school* neighborhood and an *administrative* neighborhood. It rarely occurs that all of these are identical. A physical neighborhood may be clearly defined by geographic features, or it may be entirely amorphous and depend for definition on that "neighborhood feeling" that is really a part of a social neighborhood. A social neighborhood, in general, is almost indefinable. It is small, because it depends on personal social contacts, and may be said to have a center but no boundaries. The center can be anything from a fine "community center" with its attendant activities to a saloon or a bridge table. A school neighborhood is that area which is served by a public elementary school, which may mean from 3000 to 10,000 people. An administrative unit, what the English call a precinct, might well be the same as a school neighborhood, but it is more likely to be a political ward, or some other artificially defined area.

Whatever the term may eventually come to mean, it has for planners pretty much the rather broad concept which Clarence

A. Perry has so well expressed: "It should cover both dwellings and their environment, the extent of the latter being—for city planning purposes—that area which embraces all the public facilities and conditions required by the average family for its comfort and proper development within the vicinity of its dwelling. . . . The facilities it should contain are apparent after a moment's reflection. They include at least 1) an elementary school, 2) retail stores, and 3) public recreation facilities." [2]

What is not generally understood is that the physical plan can seldom, if ever, create a "neighborhood" except in the most abstract use of the word. It can, however, very materially assist other forces in fostering a true neighborhood feeling. Nevertheless, the usual "school neighborhood" concept is too large for neighborliness and is also generally too large for private enterprise to develop properly except under rigorous planning control. Perhaps the word "neighborhood" is an unfortunate one because of its connotations and overtones. "Planning area" would have been better, for it could include, without cavil, industrial areas, business areas, residential areas, or mixtures of them. The true, social neighborhood would be a subarea within the larger one. The ideal planning area might be set up as a political-educational unit, in which the voting district (for the local legislative body), the school district, police and fire precinct, census tract, health district, and other administrative elements would be coterminous and delimited by through traffic routes, parkways, or natural geographic features. The French "arrondissement" is something of the sort, and the English idea of "precinct planning" is similar.

Many, if not all cities, have some universally recognized "neighborhoods." These are natural "planning areas" and should be retained. The County of London Plan shows how such areas are being made use of in the proposed replanning of Greater London.

The application of planning area control to the peripheries of

[2] Clarence A. Perry, *Housing for the Machine Age*. Russell Sage Foundation, 1939.

A COMPARATIVE STUDY OF LAND DEVELOPMENT

An area of approximately a square mile – As now
developed in a New Jersey city, – without benefit of
comprehensive design or land sub-division control.

Scale in feet

LEGEND

INDUSTRIAL AREA

BUSINESS AREA

RESIDENCE AREA

CEMETERIES

CHURCHES

PUBLIC OR SEMI-PUBLIC BUILDINGS

PUBLIC SCHOOL GROUNDS

PARKS

PARK
(STATE OWNED)

NEW JERSEY STATE PLANNING BOARD

PLAN "A"

160

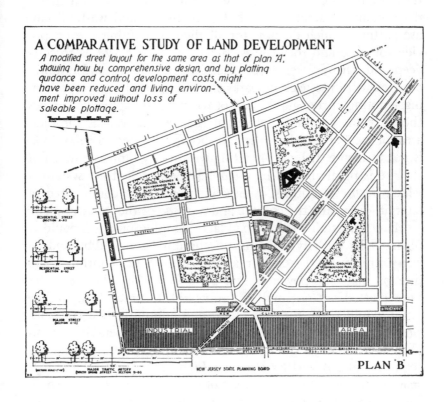

A COMPARATIVE STUDY OF LAND DEVELOPMENT

A modified street layout for the same area as that of plan 'A', showing how by comprehensive design, and by platting guidance and control, development costs might have been reduced and living environment improved without loss of saleable plottage.

NEW JERSEY STATE PLANNING BOARD

PLAN 'B'

cities and to subdivisions both within the city limits and in adjoining counties would do much to prevent a repetition of the damage done by uncontrolled development after World War I. It is not bad architecture, nor even shoddy construction that is the primary cause of blight, but uneconomic and wasteful land use patterns which do not, for all their wastefulness, even provide for civic and social uses. Blocks of such a size as to force deep and narrow lots, streets excessive in amount and undifferentiated as to use, lack of parks and playgrounds, improper zoning, ignoring of topography and of natural geographic advantages, these are the common defects of the new as well as the older areas of most cities. Very often, it should be noted, the developer is not to blame. If he is operating within city limits he may find that he is rigidly bound by a stupidly projected street system to which he must conform. This difficulty will be commented on later, in discussing the essence and purpose of the "master plan."

Many, if not all, of these bad land planning practices could be obviated by the city insisting on appropriate neighborhood design within properly set up planning areas. Strict control of subdivision plats and power to revise the City Map where land has been platted but not built upon, would do much to help. The latter would make for some legal and administrative complication, but these would not, in most cases, be insuperable. A desirable step would be to set aside land in advance for all municipal requirements. A further step would be to zone land for light manufacturing within easy range of a group of subdivisions; or, in reverse, to require adequate and well-planned subdivisions adjacent to a single large factory such as Willow Run, Dodge—Chicago, or around a group of factories. Such subdivisions would have provision for shopping centers, community facilities, and recreation according to predetermined patterns of density. Planning for integrated neighborhoods in this way is not only just good sociology, but it is also obviously good economics for the city, the worker, and the manufacturer.

The neighborhoods, or living areas, within the planning areas, should be of the latest type—free from through traffic, arranged

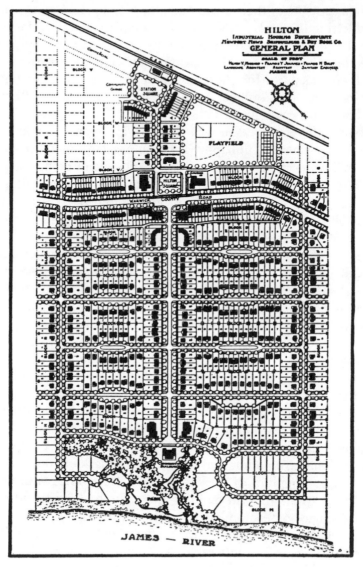

Plan of Hilton, Va., a World War I development. The severely rectangular street layout is softened and modified by the varying treatment of the set-back line for the individual houses. Francis Y. Joannes, Arch't.

for the easy use of their inhabitants for getting children to school and letting them play, for access to shopping, and with facilities for the proper functioning of democratic government by public meetings, and democratic recreation in parks and playgrounds, and with facilities for the enjoyment of such things as music, books, and other hobbies for those who want them either as audience or as participant.

Nor is there any reason why these developments should be as drab and generally unhappy as we are accustomed to seeing them. The location and general type and scale of groups of public structures—schools, shops, service and municipal buildings, churches and so on—should be predetermined and rigorously controlled. In the case of very important squares the height of adjacent structures within sight-lines, should carefully and definitely be determined. It is well to remember what the author of *Architecture in the United States* previously quoted (p. ooo) said about reciprocal duties in this connection. In closely built-up sections, some control of dwellings also might be desirable, again not as to architectural "style," but as to general broad requirements of scale and relation to the street and, in the case of row-houses, material. As has been pointed out again and again, monotony is not a function of repetition only, but of disorder. The "variety" of the row-house street which has sought to avoid monotony by using six different materials and six different types of fake gables and fancy porches, is actually as monotonous as the most excruciating street in Philadelphia or New York City's brownstones. Monotony and drabness lie in lack of composition, in the unending lines of treeless, straight streets lined with buildings built to an uniform building line. The hysterical confusion of the single-house speculative development may be just as bad, although the wider spacing and the fact there are trees and lawn is apt to make it less noticeable. An example of how this can be avoided and pleasant variety achieved at no cost at all is shown in the plan of the World-War I town of Hilton, Va. Other well-known examples of variety through careful study of the street plan and the relation of structures are Hampstead Garden

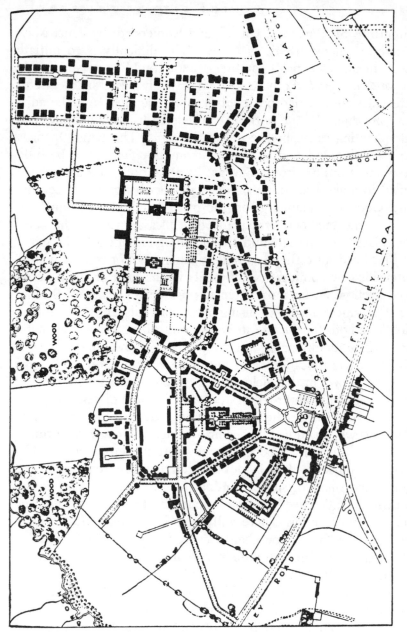

Hampstead Garden Suburb, England: A plan by Sir Raymond Unwin of great variety of treatment.

Suburb by Sir Raymond Unwin, and Römerstadt by Ernst May. There are many others, of course. The difficulty is to initiate some means of control for the sporadic building of small-scale private enterprise. Perhaps all that is really necessary is careful street design and rigorous control of public areas and the adjacent buildings. While nothing can redeem bad architecture, bad city-planning can ruin the greatest designs. The Paris Opera is an example. Designed to be seen from all sides, it can be fully seen only from the front. Garnier's protestations to the Emperor failed to make Haussmann understand or change the street layout. Good city planning, on the other hand, can do much to redeem the mediocre street and give pleasantness to the commonplace. Architecture and city planning are one and the same.

This need for esthetic as well as other types of control will be intensified by coming developments in the field of small house construction. So far most attention has been given, and the farthest advances made, in using new materials and "prefabrication" methods for the one story dwelling. Some of the new materials will unquestionably affect multi-family dwellings also, but structural complications and antique building codes will make progress slower in that field. The great emphasis is being put on the so-called prefabricated or "packaged" house of extremely low cost. This will reach the widest market, and also the newest subdivisions when and if it comes into being. There are some things about it which must be given very careful consideration. The first, of course, is the obvious danger that will come from uncontrolled small-lot subdivisioning. Multitudes of cheap houses on tiny lots, "owned" by installment-plan financing are nothing but potential slums. There will be a determined effort also to develop the "house you change every five years," or ten years— the analogy of the automobile and its annual style changes is often used—and rightly, because only by some such forced "repeating" of sales could a sufficiently large market be created to support an industry large enough to produce cheaply. However, the jalopy can be, and is, eventually run to a junk yard and scrapped; the danger with the jalopy house will be that the owner, having nothing to lose, will walk out and go elsewhere; or if he does stay and trade in the house every so often, what does the municipality get out of it? For if taxes continue to have an *ad valorem* base, the $898.87 house cannot be taxed enough to pay anywhere near its share of the cost of municipal services. True, the poor do not pay their share of such costs now; but the cheap prefabricated house is being much touted as a remedy for slums and as an argument against public housing. It is no such remedy, and contains the seeds of great danger unless it is recognized as a city-planning problem and proper controls are set up for it. These will have to include county—if not regional—control of subdivision planning, and should include methods of making not merely the so-called "owners" but the promoters and finance companies financially responsible to the local government for taxes and maintenance.

The importance of maintenance as a safeguard against blight is often overlooked. The low-income family has very little, if any, money to put into repairs and general maintenance. The first evidence of blight is the disrepair and unkemptness of an individual property; lack of paint, sagging steps, tin cans, and old tires in the yard, small but clear signs of sinking interest and eventual decay. The cheaper the house, the more it will cost to maintain, relatively, and the less the owner will be able to spend on it. Even pre-fabrication will not change the fact that extreme cheapness and shoddiness go hand in hand—for no matter how cheap the good product of the reliable pre-fabricator may prove to be, there will always be the gyp producer of a cheaper and a poorer quality which will be palmed off on the ignorant and the bedeviled. Remember, the slogan of Home Ownership still is Let the Buyer Beware . . . and the municipality, too.

Besides the ultra-cheap house, other kinds of technical improvements may affect the technique of design. This has happened in the past—the superblock for instance was made possible by the oil-burner and the electric refrigerator. They freed the placement of dwellings from immediate access to a road because they made coal and ice delivery unnecessary. Much greater flexibility of design, within the house as well as in site planning, was the direct result. If pipe line distribution of metered fuel oil is developed, or electric heating, even greater flexibility will be possible. Another possibility is the on-the-spot destruction of domestic wastes, human and kitchen, by chemical action or by bacteria. At present a city is tied down, economically and literally, to a huge iron or concrete sewer pipe. This is a problem that has received little attention, but the ingenuity of present day science should be equal to it. The savings in municipal first cost and operating costs would be enormous, and the whole concept of city planning could be completely revised if sewer systems and garbage collection could be gotten rid of. Water and gas supply piping are not difficult to handle—that is, the water distribution system is not. The main trunk supply lines are, of course, large and costly, but water costs are usually a separate item of both municipal and consumer budgets, and the systems are generally not only self-liquidating but profitable. It is the sewer system that is, actually, the guts of the problem physically and in terms of cost.

Urban redevelopment also is now generally thought of in terms of "neighborhoods" or, more properly, "planning areas." Attention is naturally centered on rebuilding slums or blighted areas, particularly with a view to improving the housing of the poor and the condition of their landlords. This, of course, is laudable. Little thought has been expended on industrial slums. Proposals for the improvement of "downtown" have usually been with an eye to maintaining land values, and have not been related either to housing or to the flight to the suburbs. However, if urban redevelopment as it is now thought of can show the way to better land uses, it will be doing a definite service to the community. Eventually the great cities will have to make drastic changes in the entire pattern of land uses, anyway, and urban redevelopment projects could be extremely valuable experimentally.

This does not mean the tearing down of everything, the abandonment of all utilities or anything of the sort. It does mean a severe reduction in population density,—that is, in gross density.

It might be well here to clear up the meaning of "density" a little. The term usually refers to the number of people per acre in a given area. The acre may be "net" or "gross." "Net" means the land within property lines, excluding streets, parks, and land used for public and non-residential purposes. "Gross" means including streets, parks, and all other land within the boundaries of the area. The smaller the area considered, the more closely net and gross approach each other; the larger the area, the reverse. What is not generally appreciated is that for very large areas— say a square mile or over, in the average city—the net residential acreage is often less than 30% of the gross. Thus it is not astonishing to find that although Manhattan has a "density" of "only" 230 persons per acre, many "net" acres have 500 and some up to 750 persons living on them. In less fantastic cities this discrepancy is not so great; and what is important in any case is the relationship of net density to the open, usable space—whether such open space is in the form of parks, streets, and playgrounds or as private yards for houses or the grounds around garden apartments. Open commercial land, such as the rear yards of business structures, parking lots, and so on, if permanent, may add to light and air, but not to amenity. Consequently, it is the density per gross acre, over fairly large areas, that is the important consideration both in city planning and in regulations for the control of density.[3]

For instance, an area of a square mile that had a population of 128,000 persons, or 200 per acre might, for proper planning, have to be reduced to 96,000 persons or 150 per acre. But the density of any given *net* acre, that is, only the land within property lines, might be as high as 600 persons if qualified by transportation, parks, schools, and other facilities in the immediate vicinity. In other words, density of population over large areas must be based

[3] For a detailed study of this important subject, see *Densities in New York City*, a Report to the Citizens Housing Council of New York, by the Committee on City Planning and Zoning, Henry S. Churchill, Chairman; William H. Ludlow, Research Assistant. Citizens Housing Council of New York. 1944. mimeo.

on the facilities within those areas, and the density of any specific piece of land is unimportant except as it affects the gross density of the planning area as a whole. To put it another way, population in the square mile could be planned, theoretically at least, to house the population by even over-all distribution using all the land or, at the other extreme, in one single thousand story structure at the center, leaving the rest open. The tax situation would be exactly the same in either case. But the kind of living would be very different and so would all the physical planning problems be different. Actually, of course, good planning will take advantage of the skyscraper to provide concentrations at strategic spots, to give variety to the uses to which land can be put, to provide for different ways of living, and to give esthetic interest to the skyline. With the exception of Manhattan and some parts of the other boroughs, no other city has population densities that are too high to be taken care of by a more intelligent use of land. The consolidation of sections of the city into superblocks, the creation of well-designed and properly located shopping centers, ample school and local recreational space, are all possible within the framework of the present density patterns of most cities.

Rationalization of land-use would, as a matter of course, restrict the amount of land used for commercial purposes, and would develop at least some relation between industry, particularly light industry, and residence. Certain cities already have the beginning of a "finger-park" system which serves as a buffer strip, for recreation, and for public structures. Rock Creek Park in Washington comes to mind; Boston has the greater part of such a system (although it does not reach into the old city); Kansas City has a highly developed system of parkways. Toronto is proposing a similar scheme, making use of its fine ravines and connecting them at the outer end, and even proposes an agricultural belt to restrain undue fringe development. The County of London Plan makes much of "green wedges" running into the city, and insists on the importance of a "green belt" of fairly unspoiled country. It makes the very important distinction between parks and country, a distinction which, of course, concerns the metropolis rather than the smaller city which has, as the medieval towns had, the country within easy reach.

Certainly, the use of such parks will do much to make our cities more livable. Green is a great help in cities, and Paris and Washington, to name only the two most conspicuous examples, owe their charm largely to trees. Incidentally, both cities owe them to "bosses"—Paris to Haussmann, Washington to Boss Shepherd. One should be grateful to the almost forgotten Boss every time one goes through that matchless stretch of arching elms on New Hampshire Avenue; no brass name plate says that these and 60,000 other trees are the monument of Alexander R. Shepherd, President Grant's Commissioner of Public Works.

The taxation-land value dilemma in relation to replanning has been touched upon, but it is not the only one. The areas in need of rehabilitation and change are so large, and the land is held in so many ownerships that both power of eminent domain and very large aggregations of capital are needed in order to assemble land and reconstruct the areas. Government would seem to be the only source of capital and it already has the power of condemnation, so that while there have been a few feelers by insurance companies to see if they could become possessed of the sovereign right of eminent domain, it is generally conceded that government should buy the land and hold the bag.

There have been, and will be, innumerable variations of the basic proposal: government acquisition of land followed by disposal at a loss to be made up by some form of subsidy. Discussions as to the method of subsidizing are complicated and legalistic, involving as they do theories of federal and local participation, agency powers, application of the subsidy and, above all, semantics.

There is further dispute as to what shall be done with the land after assemblage: shall it be held by government—local government, presumably, not federal—and leased to private enterprise, or shall it be sold off in large units under municipal control of planning and use, or shall it simply be resold? All these methods have their proponents, all have their opposition.

Most of the rooters for urban redevelopment favor the second method, selling off large units under municipal control of use, because its simplifies a good many of the problems which are inherent, in different ways, in the other two schemes. It would ensure the coming-in of the huge amounts of capital controlled by the insurance companies and other large institutions, and would make possible the floating of loans to the public by specially organized holding companies. The public control of the public interest would have to be rather vague and not too onerous, something easily pushed aside once the redevelopment company was in possession of the land and the financial interests refused to play ball unless . . . ! The poor performance of the New York City Planning Commission in the face of the Metropolitan Life's billions is not reassuring as to how far cities could maintain any decent democratic control over the extended power of huge landlords. It is not pleasant to contemplate great sections of our cities under the absolute domination of the Metropolitan Life Insurance Company, or General Motors, or the Aluminum Company of America, or Bethlehem Steel, or Sun Oil or any other uncontrolled agency. If any one concern were to get hold of even as little as one percent of a city's real estate it could, and probably would, set itself up as a super-government. No politician would dare to stand up to it.

This is not an idle danger, and makes one recoil a little from the fascination of "large scale rebuilding." Too often "large-scale" is just another way of saying that we are too lazy to work out the details of reasonable-scale democratic effort—let's hand it over to great big Mr. M. and let him run it for us. Beyond a certain, fairly well ascertainable point, there are no economies or benefits in "large scale." The laws of gravity, thermo-dynamics and diminishing returns still seem to work in spite of Einstein, air-conditioning and the believers in super-government by private enterprise. Moreover, whatever applicability "large scale" may have in its proper field of manufacture and production, it has none at all in the fields of political and social relations; it is as phony as "stream-lining" applied to electric toasters and grand pianos.

The feudalistic planning and racial discrimination of Stuyvesant Town was only one example of what might happen; it is inconceivable that we should have to tolerate private enclaves. The "company towns" of the past were, at least, completely separate entities, and moreover they were not the beneficiaries of government subsidy. Another danger that is inherent in the development of large areas on a monopolistic basis (whether it be by government or by private enterprise) is the tendency to oversimplification of the market in terms of economics or race. The segregation of the poor by USHA in "economic ghettos" was bad; the exclusion of Negroes by the Metropolitan Life is also bad, but in the controversy over Stuyvesant Town there was little attention paid to the equally obnoxious fact that this was a project to house 12,000 families of one economic level in one spot in identical warrens. Within limits, of course, economic grouping is natural and inevitable, but the grouping should be one of choice and reasonable range of income, and the number of people in any one group should not be too large, or there is great possibility of our setting up a new series of "class-areas" not too different from the days of Mohenjo-daro. Such grouping, done because it was "large scale" and easy, and because of its supposed "safety of investment of sacred trustee funds" would inevitably break down the democracy of our public school system and strike at the foundations of our social order. And, to repeat, the great public housing projects are just as objectionable in this respect.

What we lack, in considering these problems, is a sense of scale. What is tolerable in a project, private or public, of say a thousand persons, or two thousand, becomes intolerable when twelve thousand are involved. At some point along the line *public interest* becomes paramount, no matter what the financial scheme, simply because an x number of people are the public.

Another complication that has not been faced by either of these methods of approach is what to do with the population

displaced from the areas to be rebuilt. With the housing shortage that will exist as a result of the war, it will hardly be possible
for thousands of families to find satisfactory quarters elsewhere
unless they are provided beforehand. It will be silly, in fact impossible, to require, as some proposed redevelopment laws require, that displaced tenants be relocated in quarters of equal
quality and rent before demolition can commence. Who is going
to supply them, and where? And if people are once satisfactorily
located elsewhere, why should they move back? And if they
don't move back, who will fill the re-built areas? And if the rebuilt areas are filled by families coming from elsewhere in the
city, from a higher economic level probably, what happens to
the areas they leave? Perhaps it has not all been thought through.
Or perhaps the slum areas that are not "redeveloped" are to be
nicely filled up because of increased demand and their "values"
raised so that when their turn comes for redevelopment there
will be still more gravy. Perhaps it has been thought out very
well.

The third method of disposition of land, by indiscriminate
sale to small owners or to large ones, is usually attacked as lacking in any possibility of planning control and, as a corollary, a
sooner-or-later return to the present state of chaos, with nothing
gained. The difficulties of establishing control under the multi-
ownership system have already been pointed out, so that politically, legally, and financially, this seems the least desirable of the
three choices. Nevertheless it has certain merits, which are perhaps too lightly brushed aside in favor of the "large scale" procedure—principally the merit that it would really preserve private
enterprise as it was in the days of Adam Smith instead of as it is
in the days of Big Business. We talk a lot about Small Business,
and we cock a wary eye at Big Business. If we cannot control
land use and social oppression if Big Business owns the land,
and if returning the land to Small Business means continuing
chaos, we are left only the possibility of considering the third
method—continued ownership of land by government.

This is dished up as "socialization of land," and is distasteful to the general, particularly since they have never gotten used to the taste of caviar, a communistic Russian food eaten only by capitalists and excreted as fascism. Why municipal ownership of land is so stridently objected to is hard to understand. Possession under a long-term lease is secure; "due process" could apply as well to the value of the lease and to the structure as to land held in fee, brokers could still make money buying and selling and leasing; the city's fiscal problem could be much simplified, and the problem of "unearned increment" could be much more readily adjusted. Another point that is seldom considered in connection with leased city-owned land is that once the cost of the land has been amortized (that is, the bonds for its purchase retired) there is no further need for carrying this item against rents. When property is sold and resold each succeeding owner must amortize the land anew, and as a result it is always a charge against the tenants in the form of higher rents. Moreover, on a lease basis the city could work out several kinds of revenue-producing rent instead of the *ad valorem* tax. For business, industry and apartments, the lease might have a percentage-of-profits base, with a guaranteed minimum. For owned homes, a rental based on benefits—i.e. municipal services rendered. For low-rental and public housing, the rent could either be merely interest based on the capitalized use value, or an arbitrary scaled arrangement depending on the means of the people housed and the rent to be attained. In any case, complete control of land would be possible, of density, of use-distribution, and eventually, of the disposition of the structures on the land. Virtually nothing would change, except that the municipality would be in a position to execute planning and insist on orderly development, according to planning areas. The matter of "time-zoning" for the elimination and control of non-conforming uses, would be a question of length of lease. "Compensation and betterment," as our English friends call it, could be worked out over a period of years—these things take a long time—at probably no more cost to the public than the fancy subsidy schemes now being proposed for urban redevelopment. In fact, and that is the

point of this paragraph, urban redevelopment purchase and subsidy *should* be a first step towards municipal ownership of *all* the
land.

There is one very valid argument against it: the opportunities
for graft and corruption, the possibility of such political terror-
ism as exists in Jersey City. The answer to that would seem to
be, we have graft anyway—it exists whenever people fail to exercise their civil duties; it disappears when the people insist it shall
disappear. If we refuse socially desirable action because our servants may prove to be corrupt and the remedy difficult, we negate
democracy and secretly yearn for the simplicity of tyranny.

If the cities owned the land the dilemma of cartel domination
or chaos might be resolved by a wise leasing of land to all kinds
of enterprise, and for all sorts of economic and social groupings.
It could, by skillful planning, make provision for the residential
neighborhood or for industrial groups, for the small factory, for
the local voice in government, as well as for the investments of
the large financial institutions. Hans Sachs and the Guilds will
not return, but there must, if we are to progress, be a source of
new brothers Wright, new Henry Fords, new Edisons, coming
from the repair shop and the home laboratory, as well as the
anonymous geniuses in the factories and laboratories of the great
corporations. Likewise, local government and the revolution so
dear to Thomas Jefferson has always found its strength in the
bazaar, the agora, the market place, or around the cracker barrel.
The strength of the future must come from a similar source—the
windy blasts issued in Madison Square Garden, the futile flatu-
lence of the radio "forums" will not suffice. To give our cities
over to private super-governments would be to betray us; the
alternative is not to relapse into unplanned chaos, but to retain
control. If the government of the people is to be for the people,
it must be by the people.

The implication of the decentralizing process and the emphasis on neighborhood and community needs is that a new
pattern is emerging, different from but analagous to those of the
past. The feudal and religious community was walled, and cen-

tered on the castle or the cathedral; the monarchic cities were also walled, and centered on the palace; the mercantile city is unwalled but congested, and centers on the business area; the town of the future will be a series of agglomerations centering around the community building and the school, with business and industry localized in relation to living rather than the other way around. For the concept of the school is changing to meet the needs of an ageing population, which will have more leisure and desire for adult education. Properly planned and administered the school is the natural focus of the community. Its plant can be used eighteen hours a day seven days a week for education, recreation, health and assembly. The formidable aspect and unpleasant characteristics of schools as we have known them will change to openness and warmth, to service to the community instead of pedantry and superiority. They will be, in effect, the common mans' club. This may be, probably is, in the quite distant future, but all indications point to some such solution of the problems that today confront us. Democracy will be best served if we do this willingly, bending technology to the common good rather than to have it used by evil forces intent merely on saving themselves.

The replanning of cities will not be brought about in one great shot, by "urban redevelopment" or anything else. The process will of necessity be gradual, although it is likely to come about more quickly than many people think it will. The essential thing is that there must be broad planning, so that not only first things will come first, but that they go in their proper place. There are many things that we can put in the right place today, a lesser number that we properly locate for the coming five years or so, and still fewer whose placement we can guess at beyond that. Nevertheless, if there is to be orderly growth, certain far-distant possibilities must be put down in the record for guidance, and corrected as time goes on. This process is called "master planning."

A Master Plan, be it noted, is *not* a blue print. It is *not* an "official map." It is not a map at all, although parts of it may be in the form of maps. It is an accumulation of interpreted data, financial, social, physical; it consists of fact, fiction, surmise, and wishful thinking; of maps, notes, photographs, suggestions. It is, as the planners of TVA put it: *"Not one goal, but a direction. Not one plan, once and for all, but the conscious selection by the people of successive plans."*

A master plan therefore is not something static, but alive and ever-changing as circumstances change. It must be continually brought up to date, and continually kept before the public, for a master plan in which the public does not participate is not a master plan but a set of blue prints for an ivory tower.

Since no master plan, by its very definition, can be carried out as proposed by any commission, its influence can only be imposed if the direction it points is one that is acceptable to the public. This acceptability is dependent on making the public understand not the complexities of accomplishment but the simplicities of objective: the social and civic good. "This" they should be told in effect, "is our conception of what will be a livable city for all the inhabitants thereof, and a beautiful one. If you, the people, think well of it and want it badly enough, eventually you will get it, or at least its basic principles." To do this would take not only time, a lifetime of devotion in and out of office, but courage as well.

For a master plan to be of influence, it must have a direction and a philosophy—the one implies the other. Most planning commissions are so puzzled about the economics of accomplishment, so confused as to their objectives, and so scared of the real estate interests and the "practical men," that they have found no direction, much less evolved a philosophy upon which to rest, for good or ill, the foundation of their planning. They draw back from the attacks they know will be made on any long range ideas, no matter how tentatively presented, they fear the sneers of the men of immediacy. These up-and-doers are in the saddle, they have immediate objectives and need no direction since they are not going anywhere except where they are. Although they do not realize it, they are like the Red Queen, they must go twice as fast if they wish to get somewhere. Master planning is not for them. The sands of time run out too quickly.

It is also a sad fact that many planners have no sympathy with the TVA approach: they are impatient of the democratic process, suspicious of the public, disgusted by the politicians, wearied by the laws delays. They look back with longing at the great absolutist accomplishments in city planning; their training has given them admiration for the beautiful result and no distaste for the means. Perhaps that is a little unjust to most of them, they do not long for the rôle of despot, they feel only an impatience, a frustration, in the democratic process a little like that of a parent who argues with an obstinate child while longing to use force to get the matter over with, restraining themselves, urging the brat to learn for its own good. They are like Little Red Riding Hood's Pa and Ma in Guy Wetmore Carryl's poem:

> Most worthy of praise were the virtuous ways
> Of Little Red Riding Hood's Ma,
> And no one was ever more cautious and clever
> Than Little Red Riding Hood's Pa.
> They never misled, for they meant what they said,
> And they frequently said what they meant—
> They were careful to show her the way she should go,
> And the way that they showed her, she went.

Whereas a master plan is a frame of reference, a concept rather than a "plan," is not "adopted" by the local legislative body and is not legally binding, a City Plan, or "official map" such as the Holme plan of Philadelphia, the 1811 Commissioner's Map of New York, or the present-day Official Maps filed in City Engineer's offices, is a legal document, in essence rigid and in effect ultimately blighting if projected too far into the future. The purpose of the Official Map is just the reverse of the Master Plan: it records where things are, down to the last manhole. It is an absolutely necessary and indispensible document. It is when it is projected in detail too far ahead of actual ripeness of land for use that its legally binding quality constipates the city. No one can predict the detailed use of land very far in advance of need, and to lay out streets under such an illusion has always proved calamitous. Main routes and parkways can and should be determined and mapped; public areas, such as parks and school-sites come closer in time—but the actual subdivision of the land should be left to the very last. The absurdity of the projection of a city map too far ahead of the growth of the city is obvious in Philadelphia, Chicago, Manhattan, Queens, and almost every other large city where it has been done. The obliteration of the beautiful topography of Manhattan is a terrible example; the accompanying maps of an outlying section of Philadelphia (not the Holme map, but a later city engineer's brain-storm) shows how a fine outlying area was rescued, barely in time, from the same fate.

The official map should not go much beyond the public works for the immediate future—say three to five years. After that, planning should become ever more diagrammatic and flexible. It becomes master-planning—or, inversely the master plan becomes the official map as time goes on and sound proposals become realities. The same is true of the area encompassed. The city can be quite definite about what to do with a specific block or section, perhaps even with a "planning area," but as planning covers more and more of the city it must have recourse to greater generalities, i.e., to determining only those things that are essential to the city as a whole, such as main transportation routes, the establishing of planning areas, the co-ordination of facilities, probable locations for certain of these facilities, and the economies of government. The metropolitan area plan must be still more general, dealing with trends except where it can accomplish the specific task of co-ordination of the grand strategic needs of the area through its knowledge of the problems and proposed solutions to the needs of the component parts, or as it can establish definite objectives and work for their attainment. The tactics of attainment are immediate in time and local in development.

The master plan and the official city map thus represent the extremes of planning: the one a vision of things long hoped for, the other the evidence of things now seen . . . In between, a sort of bridge from one to the other, is the zoning law. If the master plan is a guide and the official map a record, zoning is an instruction and restraint. Zoning can be the most powerful tool yet devised for effectuating the purposes of the master plan. Its origin and present low estate have been previously mentioned: what is important now is the fact that the essential validity of zoning as an instrument of public welfare has been upheld by the courts. The control of land use and of building bulk has thus been established, and in some jurisdictions the direct control of density, i.e. persons per acre, as well. Within the broad frame-work of the master plan it is therefore possible to assign zones of use, bulk and density which become more and more precise and restrictive as the area zoned becomes more fully developed. A zoning law, unlike the master plan, is a series of legally adopted maps, but unlike the official map these can be varied, within reason, by a board of appeals, without recourse to the local legislative body for the variation. This gives limited flexibility. Wisely used, therefore, zoning can promote the objectives of the master plan by controlling land-uses not only in general areas, but also where necessary along particular highways or specific spots so that conformity to the master plan of transportation, for instance, would be ultimately attained.

It is a curious paradox, quite in keeping with our times, that professional planners seek to "sell" master planning on economic grounds alone, ignoring or even denying the social benefits and esthetic aspects. The paradox lies in that the alleged economic benefits become socially acceptable largely to the extent that they make for social benefits which cannot, statistically, be proven to have anything to do with city planning. A substantial rise in the level of real wages would probably solve the major economic problems of most cities without recourse to a single plan for redevelopment; current attempts to solve economic problems in terms of city planning are bound to be fruitless. Nevertheless, in an effort to be deemed sound and practical, planners talk economics instead of human welfare and civic art.

But by now it seems plain that attempts to do city planning in terms of economics alone is also fruitless. Only human welfare and beauty can stir the imagination of people, and only through the desire of people can there be accomplishment. In fact it is doubtful if democratic planning can take place at all until the incomes of people can support their purpose; plans made in the sands of a desert where the hot winds blow are illusory at best.

The great city plans of the past have all been plans which have fired the imagination. Although few of them have ever been completely carried out they have served, in a very real way, as "master plans." Wren's plan for London—an example and objective for centuries. The extraordinary redesign of Paris of which the competition for the Place de la Concorde was a part started a whole series of plans for that city, culminating in the famous "Plan des Artistes," so called, made in 1793, the fourth year of the Revolution. On it was based nearly all the building done under Napoleon I, and it gave Haussmann many of his ideas. The beautiful city of Copenhagen developed, for over a hundred years, along lines planned under Christian IV about 1600. In this country Boston still has to catch up with Robert Morris Copeland, and the Burnham plan of Chicago and the Regional Plan of New York have offered continued stimuli.

It is emphatically true that we cannot today approach city planning in the same manner that the designers approached it in the past. We do have to consider the economics of operation, and we must think in terms of living and not in terms of display. Today we plan to house millions, not a potentate and his court, and it is an altogether different problem. Nevertheless, the ultimate solution must be imaginative if it is to be accomplished. To put the reclamation of Chicago's lakefront, or the major accomplishments of Moses' park administration under the heading of "economic projects" is manifestly absurd. Yet they were built, paid for, and are maintained, at enormous cost. Why? Because of the intangible factor of civic pride which rejoices in a great work nobly done. Or, if you must put the dollar mark on it, a just balance sheet would write it off as advertising.

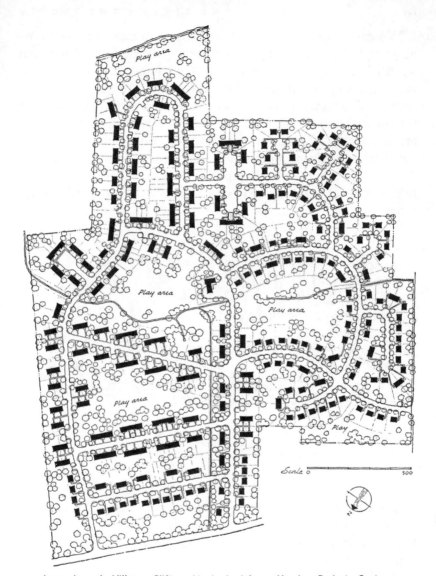

Acquackanonk Village, Clifton, N. J. A defense Housing Project. Contour planning. Superblocks, large play-areas, no through traffic, avoidance of monotony in plan although all houses are similar in material and design. Henry S. Churchill, architect.

We can if we wish bring into being any city plan that stirs us enough. By now we know that money in itself is not national wealth but only a representation of it. The creating of wealth is production, and if in war we can expend nearly all we produce for destruction, in peace we can, if we will, expend as much for construction. None of the things that are desirable in a city are impossible of achievement. The techniques of planning are adequate enough; economic lag, legal obscurantism, and public indifference are the real stumbling blocks. They can only be overcome by something that will seriously disturb public indifference.

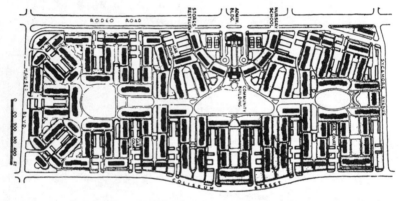

Baldwin Hills Village, Cal. The integrated superblock instead of the chopped up subdivision; possible only where a large area is designed as a unit. Reginald D. Johnson and Wilson, Merrill and Alexander, Arch'ts.; Clarence S. Stein, consulting architect.

That something is the bringing into the everyday surroundings of people the cause for civic pride that is associated today with the antiquated Grand Plan of Absolutism, but which once existed as a communal commonplace of towns. Architecture, the most ubiquitous of the arts, must again function as the moulder of the third dimension of city planning, giving coherent and beautiful form to the places in which our lives are spent.

It is perhaps not chance that the greatest progress in city planning in recent years has not been in the big cities but in the small, in new towns and projects which have nearly all been designed by architects. Letchworth and Welwyn; Römerstadt; Radburn to Baldwin Hills Village by way of the greenbelt towns and all the many experiments in the war projects, from Massena to Charleston and Norfolk, from Willow Run to Vallejo. These have been the proving grounds for the new techniques.

A new synthesis of design is sorely needed. A city plan today is the product of many diverse techniques; it is a group product, the result of team work by specialists in many fields. It is a co-operative effort, and there is therefore little feeling of individual responsibility, and likewise little pride of creation. And because of the nature of modern industrial production and construction, a city plan cannot be a genuinely communal effort, as were the medieval cities. What is needed, then, is a device by which the technical essentials of the city plan can be subordinated to the greater elements of design, something in the way the technical essentials of industrial buildings have been assimilated by architects such as Albert Kahn of Detroit and Roland Wank of TVA, leaving them free to create appropriate and beautiful form.

A great and imaginative piece of work, in any art, must present a central thesis, an idea of power; how many groups can have, and express unreservedly, a single idea? The greatest ideas in city planning in modern times have been Howard's, LeCorbusier's, and Frank Lloyd Wright's—they are ideas, not specific plans. The best plan so far is Forshaw and Abercrombie's County of London Plan, a daring but also well studied, analyzed and documented scheme which will have far-reaching effects. This, of course, is the work of many people, but the direction was by a team who, by signing their names, assumed responsibility for fighting for it and defending it. Perhaps the worst plan in recent times is Sir Edward L. Lutyens' plan for London—a plan that neglected all that had been learned since the days of Daniel Burnham. Clearly, we cannot dispense with the economics, the surveys, the traffic experts and all the rest. Just as clearly, these are not in themselves sufficient. There must be great interpretation, complete assimilation of all the composing elements into a composition that transcends them.

Does this sound like a plea for genius? One does not reach for the moon, but one can grasp a firefly. It is a plea and a warning to the many competent planners of this country to release their imaginations, unofficially if they cannot do so officially, and forget the immediate problem on their boards. It is a warning that if they do not, their work will be largely in vain, because great changes are taking place and what seemed like a shiny new statistic this morning is an inconsequent irrelevancy tomorrow. The practice of city planning consists of lines on paper and tables of figures from calculating machines. It is "adopted" if it is mediocre enough. The art of city planning is four dimensional, consisting of length, breadth, height and imagination. If it is good enough, it gets built into the culture of a nation.

Zoning, master plans, surveys—these are instruments, not ends. The end is a livable city, suited to modern technologies of living. Until the planners know by what methods the ends are to be achieved, what the purpose of the city is, what those who live in it (not just those who "own" it) want it to be, planning will continue to be merely the means of livelihood of planners. A city plan is the expression of the collective purpose of the people who live in it, or it is nothing. For in the last analysis, planning is not just yielding to the momentary pressures of fugitive groups, nor is it even the making of beautiful maps encompassing future hopes. It is something far more subtle; something inherent and ineluctable—the unspun web in the body of the spider.

EPILOGUE

I NOTED IN THE PREFACE THAT I HAVE CHANGED MY MIND ABOUT a good many things since this book was first published. Perhaps the basic change is that progress in city-planning theory and design would continue to come by way of the "new towns." I could not have been more wrong, for not only have we not had any more "new towns" (in the United States) but the ideals and goals set up by the new towners have turned out to be stultifying to clear thinking about ideals and goals for established cities.

THE NEW ENVIRONMENT

This emphasis on physical planning and design, essential to the creation of a new environment, necessarily shifted when the emphasis shifted from creation to tinkering. From "new towns" and a firm base of three-dimensional actuality, city-planning has had to concern itself with administrative action based on statistical analysis, fiscal obligations, and political suitability.

While there have been virtually no new "planned communities" since Park Forest and Levittown, there has been an immense increase in official municipal planning. The official city planner is now an honored functionary in practically every city and town of any consequence.

Outside these cities the great urban sprawl of the past decades has continued to take place, unguided and uncontrolled except by "subdivision regulations." In general, this morass of sprawl has incorporated the planning precepts of the advanced planners of 1935 without the least understanding of what were the real principles involved. Thus they use curved streets on flat land, occasional changes in set-back alignment, two sets of road-widths. Even "greenways" to the school are common, and all the larger developments have their little shopping-centers with pedestrian mall, and many have the come-on of a little community swimming-pool, heavy with chlorine and race prejudice.

They are, for all their faults, better than the raw-land subdivisions of the '20s—but why shouldn't they be, for at least there are houses, paved streets and sewers (or septic tanks!). The device of FHA financing, which effectively put an end to the dismal procedures of the '20s, has provided people with places which are livable, for the moment. What will happen when the inevitable deterioration of the houses sets in, remains to be seen. But it is extremely doubtful if the immense production of houses in the last decades could possibly have been done on a more structurally sound basis, and it is extremely doubtful whether "permanency" is really desirable. It will be easier, in the future, to tear down the wooden shacks than to tear down something soundly built. That the owner has, in the meantime, paid over twice the cost in interest need not concern us.

What is unfortunate is that there has been no progress in the design of these communities or developments as physical entities. One should not expect too much, but it is not too much to expect some progress, somewhere, since Levittown, New York. Apparently nothing better has been thought of. The creative mental process seems to have atrophied since Stein and Corbu. I have given what I think are some reasons for this, but even in England the New Towns are mostly a putting together of the leftovers of Garden City and *la Ville radieuse*. However in England they look at their past and do learn something—Crawley New Town is not Letchworth. Sharp, Gibberd, Holford and others have gotten out text-books and critical articles, made detailed comparisons of design and theory. We in this country have done nothing of the kind.

THE NEW MYSTIQUE

In the United States the necessities of official "justification" and our peculiar *penchant* for the mystical have greatly over-stimulated all aspects of statistical data gathering. This is especially true in economic and social city-planning. We not only know how many pins are manufactured, but how many angels dance on their heads. As I noted many years ago, this satisfies the American businessman's belief in quantification. If it bears the label "exhaustively researched" he inquires no further. The members of Planning Commissions are businessmen. They cannot go behind the competency of their staff. To put a final—I hope—twist to the old gag, what is good for IBM is good for the city.

One study, for example, has piled up over 8,000,000 IBM cards. From them you can tell how far apart Service Stations should be to service little three-year old Mary on family outings. In France it's simpler—the Roadsides are for People. The Director of this study rightly points out that these cards provide basic information about peoples' travel habits and many other things. They should be continuously added to so that from them almost any type of selective planning data could be obtained for use in the region. All that is lacking is theory to which to apply the data, theory which in some way pertains to the solution of the human problems of regional growth and change.

This is all part of our time. Numbers produced fission and fusion. Sociologists and others look for support from Numbers. With the anthropologists gnawing at their bones on one side and the psychiatrists biting at their intuitions on the other, Numbers are a last recourse. Numbers result in an equation: quantification equals dehumanization: the city is not the people.

COMPREHENSIVE ZONING

Planners have greatly improved their status in municipal affairs. The Planning Commissions in almost all the larger cities and many of the smaller ones are charged with budgetary planning. Departmental budgets which contain items of capital expenditure are subject to the coordinating powers of the Commission, which assigns them priorities in accordance with a five or six year program of public works. This part of Planning Commission activity has been very successful. It has brought continuity and coordination to scattered and rival proposals, and provides the Mayor, the local legislative body and the department heads with a standard over-all view.

This procedure is supposed to tie in with what used to be called the Master Plan and is now usually called the Comprehensive Plan. Only a comparatively few cities have a Comprehensive Plan. The budgetary capital plan therefore becomes in itself a sort of comprehensive plan, or master plan, often based on material that is intended to be used, some day, for a complete Comprehensive Plan. The long-range physical intentions derive from the zoning maps, despite all legal theories to the contrary.

Philadelphia has recently (1961) completed its Comprehensive Plan. It supersedes a Comprehensive Plan of 1917, long and well forgotten. It remains to be seen whether the work of the Commission will be facilitated by it and whether its existence will have any effect whatsoever on any action of City Council, particularly as to the legislating of zoning variances. This is a field which is everywhere particularly sensitive to "pressure."

Because of this sensitivity, zoning has failed as a "tool" for carrying out planning. The urgency for zoning brought about its adoption by cities and towns long before they did any long-range planning. This was necessary in order to freeze the status quo, more specifically to try and keep Negroes and poor people out. Once adopted, the escape valves to the code are always used to "downgrade" property, never to "upgrade" it, since "upgrading" is never profitable. The procedure is somewhat as follows:

an option is obtained on a piece of land in a vulnerable location and an application is made to the board of adjustment for a downgrading of the property, known as a "variance." If the variance is granted, he can build more units on it, or use it differently, and he has an automatic profit on the land. If he doesn't get it, he can still appeal to the local legislative body for a complete change in the zoning. If he gets it, he makes his profit as before. If he doesn't get it he loses nothing but whatever it was he contributed to the coffers of The Party. This is, in any case, almost his entire investment, because if he is forced to build there are various subsidizing agencies to finance him.

This crudely described process and its variations are the kind of thing that the shrewdness of speculative enterprise can squeeze out of the best-intentioned legislation. It is one of the reasons why zoning is now so well supported by real estate and builders. It brings out their ingenuity—a study of such gimmicks would make entertaining reading.

Since zoning is not a very good method of control from the point of view of the planner, there would seem to be no really satisfactory way of making things come out the way they should short of actual government ownership of land. This, as a permanent measure, is still looked at askance, although not so fearsomely as it used to be. The Urban Renewal process has taught the municipalities a good deal, and some cities now talk openly about a "Land Bank." This, however, will not really be municipal ownership of land. The city will just "bank" it until it is needed by some favorite son at the right price.

THE TRANSMOGRIFICATION OF SLUM CLEARANCE

While city planning has greatly improved the political control of speculation in land, there has taken place an almost parallel loss of social purposes.

It had become evident that slum clearance could not be achieved solely by Public Housing. It was necessarily a limited program, and administrative procedures in Washington limited it still more. The Act itself was not too restrictive, but the Administrators were unimaginative and timid. They were terrorized by the thought of Congressional investigation long before Mc-Carthy. The program had many enemies, and while its supporters were fervent they were not very powerful. They made the serious mistake of thinking they could fortify their position by forcing "projects" down the slums of dozens of places that were not particularly anxious for them.

Consequently the program met with increasing disapproval. The visible products were in general so drab, so nondescript and so ineffectual that no one would fight for them. When it became evident that social and civic benefits did not come up to expectations, no amount of "public relations" could prevent actual hostility.

Characteristically, instead of making basic changes in the program, the proponents of slum clearance blamed their troubles on the limited physical extent of the program. If slums were to be cleared in 20 years, Public Housing must become merely a part of a great effort to rebuild vast areas of our cities. The Flight from the City must be halted. It was a magnificent dream, the new frontier turned inwards, trains of Conestoga wagons hauling people back into town.

All this, the planners said, could easily be done if we set out to do it. To be effective we must not only clear residential slums but also industrial and commercial depressed areas. Total replanning was absolutely necessary and arbitrary powers would be needed to do it.

URBAN RENEWAL

The amazing fact is that legislation purporting to effect such a program was passed by the Congress. It was included in the amendments to the Housing Act of 1949 and subsequent amendments. In simplified terms it provided that, upon certification by the local legislative body as to the slumminess of an area, the United States would advance funds to a duly authorized local body for studies of the area, for the acquisition of land, and a permanent donation of two-thirds of the difference between acquisition cost and re-sale receipts. It also extended to the local operating body far-reaching powers of eminent domain, powers hitherto carefully protected by the courts.

There were also excellent provisions regarding the relocation of displaced families, but nothing even remotely adequate for the losses incurred by the displacement of small business. Minor matters included enactment of state enabling legislation, mumblings about conformance to large-scale ("comprehensive") plans and so on. Public Housing was not to be privileged, the operating bodies were not to undertake actual construction, Private Enterprise was to be the Main Spring, the Watch Word, the Primum Mobile.

All this required a new Agency: the Urban Renewal Agency. This was welcomed as a hopeful new start against the hidebound and reactionary Public Housing Administration. The new URA was headed by excellent, idealistic young administrators who promptly got bogged down in paper-work: standards, forms, directives, regional offices, controls, reviews, re-reviews, approvals, papa-knows-bestism. This sort of thing seems inevitable —for I know that when these men took office they were against all of it and wanted very much to run a clean-cut and simple operation. They could not do it.

One reason for this, it must be said in extenuation, was the incompetency of many—far, far too many—of the professional plans submitted. Some were just plain incompetent, others were deliberately short-cut in order to get away with as little work as possible, still others bore obvious earmarks of having been done by hacks in the interest of interested parties. Some sort of basis for uniform judgment had to be established—after all, it *was* the taxpayer's money that was being used—and that was the end of good intentions. It is no more possible to be a little bit bureaucratic than to be a little bit pregnant.

POLITICAL GRIST

Another interesting thing about the early years of the program is how quickly it was accepted. The politicians in City

Hall found the prospects of a two-thirds Federal grant to be irresistible. They were not quite sure how it could be manipulated, but they were plenty sure they could find out, and the patronage prospects were enormous. The public too was receptive. Who could be against slum clearance, particularly if the slum dwellers were to be cleared away too? All this without a cent of cost to the city, because the increased revenue from rebuilding would really lower taxes and the city's one-third contribution could be in the form of routine improvements that would have to be built anyhow—sewers, libraries, hospitals, incinerators, just so they related to the "redevelopment area." There was no deliberate deception in this: just our native optimism.

For we are optimists. The Redevelopment Program was set up in the sincere belief that private enterprise would rush in and rebuild, that given the magic formulas of "write-down" and "eminent domain," investors in real-estate would be persuaded that the normal processes of real-estate speculation were no longer effective. What the promoters of the Program had either overlooked, forgotten, or never knew was that there no longer was, and had not been for many years, such a thing as private enterprise investment in the real-estate market. The various Federal agencies concerned with residential promotion had seen to it that capital need not be risked, nor in most cases even ventured. Moreover, it had been FHA policy to encourage suburban building and to discourage urban building, particularly apartments. As for commercial building, there had been almost no market. In the largest cities, a few "name" high-rise buildings had been built, but small-scale construction was almost nonexistent.

The result, which could have been foreseen, was an almost completely stagnant market for local redevelopment land in the medium and smaller cities. The "big plans" were too big, even when small, for local capital to absorb, and outside big operators naturally just were not interested. What was left was a meager crop of public buildings, city halls, court-houses, fire-houses, and such-like. This left a lot of cities sitting on the rubble of their cleared areas and quite a lot more sitting on their plans with nothing done.

In the bigger cities there was a lot of yowling on the area fences by a couple of fat cats. For a while it looked as though they might actually redevelop a major part of the United States. But this did not come about, either. No one not an expert in the intricacies of real-estate manipulation can tell the inside story of why the cream soured so fast. It should some day make a fascinating book.

NEW TENDENCIES FROM ABROAD

Meanwhile, there are indications of new tendencies in planning. They are not yet strong enough to be called trends. They are dual: deriving on the one hand from what planners have seen in Europe and, on the other hand, from what some architects have been cautiously working out here.

The paraphrases of European efforts come from the mystique of the Middle Way of Swedish conservative radicalism—i.e. common sense—which so fascinated the planners in their search for an answer to the squeals of "Socialism." Sweden, even more than England, seemed to provide the accomplishment of orderly city growth in a framework of social enterprise that was not anticapital. First the success of the cooperative housing projects and then the brilliance of Vällingby showed what could be done by private enterprise under state control. When, after the war, the huge remodeling of central Stockholm (the Centrum) was undertaken, the Swedish triumph was complete.

Swedish planning was not especially original except in its success. In the background was *la Ville radieuse* and St. Dié, in the foreground Rockefeller Center and also Rotterdam just rising from the Nazi razing. The Centrum was not an answer to housing. It was an attempt to meet serious problems of "downtown" congestion. The sensitive genius of Sven Markelius devised a plan which tied a new pattern in with an existing one, made use of local shopping customs, added to mass transport facilities and, following the example of Rockefeller Center, wasted not a square foot of space while providing ample room for pedestrian movement. That the excellently sited and privately built skyscrapers are hideous is a failure of architecture, not of planning.

Rotterdam has been completely rebuilt according to a plan that predetermined the size and shape of everything. It is perhaps because of that rigidity that it seems artificial and dull, particularly so when contrasted with the seething life and variety of Amsterdam.

The third example is Coventry. In Coventry the vehicular circulation seems to be entirely satisfactory, but the city center is a negation of good commercial planning. It has no focus, it is multi-level to no purpose, and is consequently difficult to shop in.

It is from these three major rebuildings that most of our downtown and Central City "renewal" plans have taken their cues. Our designers propose multi-level plazas of some sort, an inward-turning of space, a repellent and repelling formal organization of "cafes" and "open-air folk-dance platforms" in the resultant "plaza," and other things we are not accustomed to. They feature open-air markets of a sort no American housewife would go near, and places of amusement for juveniles that the cops would never tolerate. Sometimes these dreams are attached to Civic Centers, not intimately and closely as in Stockholm, but distantly and grandly. In Stockholm the Old Market—open-air, non-packaged, variegated, noisy, dusty, colorful—occupies the square in front of the Concert Hall. In front of the Concert Hall is Milles' delightful fountain, and the new Centrum angles off this square and becomes part of it. The packaged-food supermarket is in a lower level of the new complex and does a wonderful business, but the Old Market keeps right on too.

In the belief that several wrongs make for right, it may as well be noted that the English have given in to Progress in other ways besides the center of Coventry. They have lost the battle of the High-rise: the huge Barbican Project near St. Paul's is high-rise multi-level. It will completely ruin circulation over a wide area. They have permitted the building of a great structure near the Tate Gallery which dwarfs the Houses of Parliament and Big Ben when seen from the bridges. It seems fair to predict that within ten years there will be Expressways cutting through the heart of The City, through Hyde Park, along the Embankment, perhaps even a 3-level interchange at Lambeth Palace—all to relieve the traffic generated by new skyscrapers. Too bad, but there goes London.

NEW TENDENCIES OF OUR OWN

The other tendency I mentioned stems from indigenous notions of how to make money, which is a hopeful limb to stem from. This is the Shopping Center, which has developed and changed in character from the neighborhood prototypes of 20 years ago. The new Centers are important because they seem to work, and because they work they are beginning to affect the growth of the areas in which they are built. Moreover, some of the principles of their design are being used by imaginative architects (and clients) in already existing commercial areas. The new centers are not just places where you can buy something conveniently. They are places where you can spend your time having a pleasant time. Once you have parked your car and gotten out of the air, you don't have to get back into it. The whole combination of shops, from big department stores to food-stores to specialty shops, of various-priced restaurants, of decorative plazas and children's amusement areas, is all under one vast air-conditioned series of roofs. There are trees, sculpture, lights, moving people; everything is clean, packaged, polished, sanitized, deodorized, the American woman's dream. The big "market hall" space is used for concerts, recitals, dances, meetings on evenings and off days. The people love them, flock to them.

The surrounding area develops because of this activity. It does not conform to neat planning precepts, it is sprawl, all right—or all wrong. It acts against all ideas of green-belts or neighborhoods centered on the PTA.

That is half of the tendency I spoke of. The other half of it is the discovery that many types of activities can be advantageously combined under one sweeping roof is now being applied to downtown. There are instances, more and more each year, of the structures on an entire city block being reorganized into a single coordinated unit. A typical example would be the joining together, even the intersection, of a department store, a hotel, a parking garage, with perhaps a new arcade cut through the block to make for easier pedestrian circulation.*

There are also new buildings being designed along these lines.

This is successful urban renewal. This is making use of existing assets. This does not create a vacuum that is difficult to fill. This does not destroy. Admittedly it does not clear any slums, but it does help prevent "blight." It cannot be applied to every block, but it is a method of rejuvenation quite different from the visions of the planners who have been fascinated by the European ideas referred to previously. It is probable that it will be more satisfactory, given time, simply because it is based on our principles of investment and merchandising. These are not "better" or "worse" than foreign methods: it is just that they are based on the way we are used to doing things.

QUESTIONS OF ETHICS

The absurd process of tearing things down before there is any economic demand for replacement is more and more being brought into question. So too the wisdom of "the big plan" which will "rebuild the area" and "capture the imagination" is being questioned—or at least the wisdom of trying to put such plans into effect all at once is being questioned, since they do not seem to capture the imagination of investment capital.

Investment capital has indeed found occasional use for Urban Renewal, but not quite according to the intent of the framers of the laws. Large corporations wanting to get hold of a site on which to put a' building, influential individuals looking for

---

* A very early example of this is Grand Central Terminal, an extremely complex series of uses and structures that, with all its ramifications, could not be built under today's zoning.

a good deal, and even Educational Institutions seeking to expand, have been able, in complaisant jurisdictions, to get the local powers to use Eminent Domain for their special benefit, forcing a reluctant owner to sell regardless of whether or not there were well considered and pressing plans for Renewal. This pernicious practice has not yet been sanctified by the courts, probably because the cost of carrying a case to at least the highest State court is far in excess of what a small owner can afford.

WISHFUL THINKING

We are, we always have been, a slogan-happy nation. In 1945 our population curve was going to drop, to everyone's dismay; in 1962 it is going to rise like an anti-missile missile. In 1945 our builders were not taking care of Large Families; in 1962 we are all out to house the Silver Hairs among the Gold. The discussion of population forecasts at the end of Chapter 4 is as wrong as could be, but it was based on the demographic data current at the time. The Comprehensive Plans for cities today are being based on today's current data. There can be no objection to such procedure, for there is no other data available. The difficulty is of another sort. If there is insufficient data, or data which is reasonably unreliable by its nature, then plans which must rely on such data for their chief support ought not be formulated.

Nor are population data the only weak link in Comprehensive Planning. Land-use patterns are in part based on industrial growth forecasts; the trends for Central Business Districts, for suburban commercial needs and for supersonic highways are likewise based on guesses about the future economic state of the nation.

It follows that most Comprehensive Planning is wishful thinking. Even if the forecasts should prove to be largely correct, as well they might, there are no controls by which the distribution of people and land can be made to conform to the Plan. The Plan is therefore considered "flexible," and subject to revision to fit the facts as they evolve over the years. This, of course, is what has always happened. Plans are made and parts are carried out. Then the Plan drops out of sight and life goes on until someone thinks there ought to be another plan.

It would be instructive to dig up these old plans. They are not hard to find, they exist in the cellars of City Halls, in library stacks, in the files of architectural magazines.

Some cities have had three or even four officially proposed plans. They are instructive because nearly always they show a lot of things that fortunately were never done. They also, of course, show what the city was like before a lot of things were done, and some of the things that were done were excellent, for which the citizens should be duly grateful. Also some proposals seem perennial; they appear on all the plans and are never carried out. It would be interesting to know why.

The makers of Comprehensive Plans look forward wishfully, but they do not look back critically. It seems to me they should. There are lessons to be learned. The successes and failures of previous plans represent, in a very large measure, what is the true relation of planning theory to practice, of planning ideas to public and political acceptability. An analysis of the whys and wherefores of the success or failure of these plans should serve many purposes. This would require research into old newspaper files and other contemporary sources.

LOOKING BACKWARD

It is necessary to look back in order to go forward. Besides providing reference points as to direction, hindsight teaches many lessons. In the *Journal of the American Institute of Planners* for August 1961 Dr. William L. C. Wheaton points out that "Half a century ago, American literature offered amazingly bold visions of an egalitarian society of the future. Henry George's *Progress and Poverty*, Edward Bellamy's *Looking Backward*, and Herbert Croly's *Promise of American Life* may be cited as examples of utopian concepts that stirred the nation, set broad political movements into motion, excited the popular imagination. Today we seem largely fearful of the future, committed to lesser goals, afraid of 1984."

We would do well, I think, to review this aspect of prophecy along with the purely city-planning concepts of the past. For the works referred to are concerned with people and their future, and, as Wheaton phrased it, an egalitarian society. This too was the concern of Ebenezer Howard and his precursors and his followers—both in England and in the United States. The planning literature of today (this is a debased use of the word "literature") is concerned almost entirely with statistical averages and with statistics as "science." This leads away from the difficulties of reality into as fanciful a realm as was ever inhabited by theological scholiasts.

A MOST INGENIOUS PARADOX

It is a paradox that the idea of planning for the average always results in authoritarian controls for enforcement by the few. This has been no less true of theological presumption than of political utopianism; indeed it is the moral of the myth of Procrustes. To make everyone average in order to fit an Average of any kind requires authority to cut down or stretch out. (Remember too, it is always *your* average, not the other fellow's.) People are of various sizes, and they have various needs, interests, desires, hates and loves. They are irrational, intuitive; they like sex, money, fun. They do not all want the same thing, particularly when they are told they should have it.

It would seem therefore that cities should be designed not for the average but for the extremes. That takes a lot of imagination as well as a lot of trouble.

Nobody should have to live in an unsanitary slum. But that is an economic problem which could be solved by purely economic action. It has little to do with city planning. It has been our efforts to redress economic wrong by "city planning" that has gotten us into such a mess of political and ethical difficulties. The mixing of physical development with social purpose has resulted in economic exploitation and political deals in which the social purpose has been lost. Worse, some ancient protections of the pursuit of happiness have gone down the drain or been seriously weakened.

What is now needed is a return to a direct and singular approach to city planning. City planning is not slum clearance (social service) nor fiscal solvency (tax reform) nor the achievement of a righteous goal (honest government). City planning is the production of physical order and amenity—a three-dimensional frame for the multitude of activities of people. What goes on within the frame may be chaotic, ordered, brightly lit, lewdly conceived, dourly preached. City planning is not a part of the Miltonic moral order.

THE SPIRIT OF MAN

Yet it has a by-product of importance for the spirit of man. It may, indeed it is likely to, produce esthetic betterment. With our increasing awareness of our surroundings, with increased leisure to look, pleasantness has become an asset. Not the least of the attractions of the shopping centers is their visual appeal —not just the visual appeal of formal, organized "beauty" but the fortuitous appeal of movement, lights, displayed merchandise, squawk-boxes and radio, an ambient, in other words, rather than a studied design.

There are "projects," too, that will perhaps—if they are built —create pleasant spaces without being frigid and empty. That will be fine. In the meantime we must take care not to lose our places of real life—our Times Squares and Piccadilly Circuses, our neon-lighted Main streets and our seething Oxford streets. If we can keep these (and their counterparts in all cities and towns) great civic creations will appear in due course, although we cannot command them. We may not even recognize them. Our grandchildren will admire them and praise us, as we admire and praise the works of the past. There is always another generation snapping at our heels. Beauty, like the city, is always in process. So perhaps the chief purpose, though not the objective, of city planning, should be to provide a setting in which anything can happen. The objective should be that, within this setting, the creative genius of the few can find a way to benefit the many.

ANNOTATIONS

When we look at some of the plans of ancient cities we should be filled with wonder: not at what they managed to do, but at what we have failed to improve upon.

In a discussion about trends and the international scene, there was no mention of Africa. In 1945 we were not conscious of Africa. How quickly things change—in scope, but not in comprehension.

A reference on page 154 to Saarinen is to Eliel.

The brief discussion of the eastern seaboard metropolitan industrial complexes did not foresee the vast coverage of fusion. Not that it matters, for there the target is. The whole area, from Boston to Washington, is the subject of a remarkable and penetrating study by Dr. Jean Gottmann, "Megalopolis," undertaken for, and published by, the 20th Century Fund.

The reference on p. 168 to chemical sewer systems still entrances me. A Foundation spending a few millions on this could do more to revolutionize site planning and regional development than any other single research, but not one of them has ever even looked into it.

The generalizations about the Big Landlords (p. 172–4) have been pretty well borne out. New York City itself is now a huge slum-holder as well as a Public Housing landlord. And Metropolitan Life now wants city cops to take care of its projects.

I couldn't have been more wrong than I was about zoning—p. 181. The Epilogue gives my second thoughts.

P. 128 about regimentation: in a swank new project in Washington's Southwest, you must take the window drapes the Sponsor sells you—for esthetic regimentation. A southern Public Housing project, however, allows its female Negro tenants two illegitimate children but its female white clients only one, a new advance in moral regimentation.

FINIS

HENRY S. CHURCHILL

The late HENRY S. CHURCHILL was one of the leading
thinkers and practitioners in the field of city planning.
He was born in Chicago, studied architecture at Cornell
University, and then moved to New York, where he
combined architecture and city planning and worked
on many large-scale housing developments. He was connected with the Resettlement Administration on the
Greenbelt Towns and later acted as consultant to the
United States Housing Administration. Mr. Churchill
also practiced in Philadelphia, where he set up the East-
wick Project. He was a Fellow of the American Institute
of Architects and a member of the American Institute of
Planners, and contributed many articles to professional
journals.